Book 3 ⋈ American Aircraft Series

RYAN GUIDEBOOK

Fifty years of Ryan airplanes (1925/1975) described in detail, including the classic S-T, the PT-22, Spirit of St. Louis, Bluebird, Navion and Broughams.

by Dorr B. Carpenter and Mitch Mayborn

Front cover color photography by William Wagner, Ryan Aeronautical, 1940

FLYING ENTERPRISE PUBLICATIONS

3164 Whitehall • Dallas, Texas 75229

Library of Congress Catalog Number 75-1687
ISBN No. 0-912470-23-2 Hardback
ISBN No. 0-912470-18-6 Paperback

© Dallas, Texas, 1975 by
Flying Enterprise Publications.
All rights reserved.
2nd Edition, Revised 1976

ACKNOWLEDGMENTS: You cannot publish a book of this scope without lots of help. A book of this sort is greater than the sum of its parts and many have contributed much to it. We would be remiss (and have a hard time getting a hot supper) if we did not first thank our wives, **Elizabeth Carpenter** and **Corinne Mayborn** for their patience as we write the book and work with the airplanes.

William Wagner 1942

William Wagner took the photograph opposite the title page, this page and page six and many of the other photographs throughout this book. Through his unstinting digging into the files of the Ryan Aeronautical Library we are able to present many new facts and photos.

Robert J. Stewart of the Teledyne-Ryan Aeronautical Photo Lab has taken special efforts to see that the photographs supplied by William Wagner for this book were of high quality. We would like to extend special thanks to one of the "unsung heros" who assure the best reproduction and who seldom get credit.

Dorr Carpenter brings to this book a wealth of practical experience seldom found in historical writing. He has over 700 hours in Ryan airplanes and those he has owned include one PT-22 and S-T series airplanes c/n 355, 104, 198, 476, 456 and 177. He presently owns and flies c/n 177 which he rebuilt from a wreck. Dorr learned to fly in high school and currently holds a Commercial license with Instrument rating and a DC-3 type rating. Presently in general aviation, he is a licensed A & P mechanic and worked for United Airlines in that capacity for seven years. Dorr once flew an STA from Chicago to Nassau and an STM over 1100 miles across the Australian outback. He graduated from St. Lawrence University in 1951 and was an infantry Lieutenant in Korea. Dorr's wife is Elizabeth and his three children are Strachan, Diana and Ethan.

RYAN GUIDEBOOK

Fifty Years of Ryan Airplanes (1925/1975)
8 through 44

The Old Advertising Section
45 through 72

The Early Ryan Airplanes	73
The S-T	85
The Export STM	89
Far East Ryans	90
Saga of c/n 476	92
Ryans in Museums	107
The ST-3, PT-21, PT-22, NR-1	108

APPENDIX

Production Tables

Early Ryan Airplanes	79
B.1 Brougham	79 & 81
B.3 Brougham	81
B.5 Brougham	81
SCW Series	107

S-T Series
c/n 101 through 141	95
c/n 142 through 183	97
c/n 184 through 322	98
c/n 323 through 406	101
c/n 407 through 514	103

ST-3 Series — Known Surplus Sales
N11X through N47539	111
N47540 through 53021	113
N53022 through N99994	114
Canadian	114

Scale Drawings

B.1 Brougham	76
STA	84
SCW	105
FR-1 Fireball	116
Performance Tables	119

Mitch Mayborn was born in Temple, Texas in 1936, and in addition to being the author or co-author of seven aviation books and many articles, is a Commercial and Multi-engine pilot with Instrument rating and a licensed Airframe and Powerplant mechanic. He owns Ryan STM-S2 c/n 476, N7779. Mitch is owner of Flying Enterprise Publications and originator of the American Aircraft Series, of which the RYAN GUIDEBOOK is Book 3. He spent two years with Dresser Industries, Inc. as a corporate pilot flying the G-159 Gulfstream and the Convair 240. He lives in Dallas with his wife Corinne and Children, Ellen, Susan and Neal. He is a member of the Antique Airplane Association, the EAA, AAHS, CAHA and the Texas Aviation Historical Society.

Paul Matt, who provided the detailed drawings of the SCW, STA, Brougham and FR-1 was raised in Cincinnati, Ohio. He served as an aerial photographer with the U. S. Navy. Getting his education through the Navy and I. C. S. Paul worked as a commercial and industrial photographer, but left that to become head model builder for an engineering firm. Paul started his HISTORICAL AVIATION ALBUM series in 1967

Other fellow historians that we would like to thank include, alphabetically H. G. Anderson, Erwin J. Bulban, Everett Cassagneres, Paul Clark, Bill Hodges, Joseph Juptner, Burton Kemp, Gregory Kohn, Leo Kohn, William T. Larkins, Harold G. Martin, Paul Matt, Jay Miller, Bill Richards, USAF Museum (Charles G. Worman, Mrs. Ruth Hurt), John Underwood, Ken W. Wilson and James Young.

Foreword

RYAN AIRPLANES evoke a mystique, a feeling if you will, that tells of flying at its elemental best. From the first dusty M-1's, to the silver STA's, through the Spirit of St. Louis and all that it stands for, to the slick RPV's of tomorrow, Ryan airplanes have stood for quality, performance and emotion.

People do not look at Ryan airplanes without emotion. They do not fly them without emotion and they certainly do not write about them without emotion. Joy. Sadness. Anger and elation. These are all emotions. Ryan airplanes have all of these . . . . and more.

We have tried to tell the story of the airplanes. The airplanes. Not the men, the companies, the finances involved. Just . . . . the airplanes. William Wagner, a former vice-president of The Ryan Aeronautical Company wrote, "RYAN, THE AVIATOR" published by McGraw Hill, 1971 as THE definitive book on T. Claude Ryan and the people who built the Ryan companies. He also wrote, "RYAN BROUGHAMS AND THEIR BUILDERS" published by Historical Aviation Album, 1974 which tells more of the men and events around the airplanes.

That Ryan airplanes symbolize "flying utopia" was recognized early, as the above illustration by Clayton Knight first printed in MODERN FLIGHT by Cloyd P. Clevenger in 1941 shows. William Wagner's photograph opposite the title page conveys the same feeling. And it is the same feeling people get in 1930 and in 1975 and in 1980 when they see an old "Ryan" airplane.

Smell oil and gasoline. Feel the hot summer sun and the chill of altitude and of the wind rippling your skin. Listen to the wires hum when you read about these airplanes, for these are but empty pictures and hollow facts if you don't.

Mitch Mayborn

| Ryan "Standard" | Airliner | 9 aircraft, 1922-1925 |

The first ten airplanes operated by T. Claude Ryan included a mixed bag of surplus World War I airplanes. There were several JN4-D Jenny's, a Thomas Morse Scout and six Curtiss J-1 Standards. These were Ryan's first attempts at improving existing aircraft and the modifications varied from minor to extensive with the Standards getting most of the attention. The fuselage gasoline tank was given an airfoil shape and moved to the top of the wing as is evident in the photograph of the no. 10 airplane, named El Condor del rio Mayo. With a 150 hp Hispano-Suiza V-8 engine of French design replacing the 100 hp Hall Scott, performance with four passengers and a pilot exceeded that of the original aircraft.

| Ryan "Cloudster" | Airliner | (1 modified, 1925) |

Ryan needed a larger airplane for the Los Angeles-San Diego Air Line and found an ideal aircraft for conversion in the huge Douglas Cloudster. Built in 1920 by Donald Douglas (c/n 1) for a non-stop flight across the U.S.A., the Cloudster sported a 56 ft wingspan, was 37 ft long and had a Liberty engine of 400 hp. After one attempt in 1921 and after the U.S. Army accomplished the trip in 1923, Douglas' partner lost interest and the Cloudster was sold. Ryan acquired the airplane third-hand, assigned it c/n 9 and converted it into the flagship of the airline with 10 plush seats, cabin lights, carpet and ashtrays for the passengers. In 1926 the Cloudster was pressed into service carrying beer in Mexico. During a night charter between Tijuana and Ensenada the airplane was landed in the water instead of the beach. It turned over, and waves totally demolished it during the night.

M-1 (Wright-Hispano A-150) 6 + 1926, 1927

T. Claude Ryan flew his first original design, the M-1 parasol monoplane on its first flight February 14, 1926. The photo above records this memorable event. The first production monoplane in the USA, the M-1 was built before the time of the ATC and received a "patent" instead — No. 1,754,529. The flat sided fuselage of the M-1 was a distinctive feature of these first planes. Five unsold Hisso powered M-1's were purchased by a customer who had intended to use them for a revolution in Mexico. These were impounded by the U. S. Attorney — four were returned soon (these were re-engined and sold) but the fifth was held for the trial. When it was returned it was in terrible shape and was rebuilt and sold to Menasco Motors of Los Angeles and they experimented with a 250 hp Salmson-Menasco WWI water-cooled engine converted to air cooling by Menasco.

M-1 (Wright Whirlwind J-4B) Airmail transport 9 built, 1926-1928

The Wright Whirlwind powered M-1 was the most widely produced and most successful of the basic M-1 versions. The M-1 which was designed to carry mail and/or two passengers in an open cockpit beneath a "parasol" wing with the pilot seated behind, was the first production monoplane in the USA. With doors in the side for easy access, the rugged M-1 proved just the airplane for the fledgling Pacific Air Transport. PAT which operated seven Wright powered M-1's, later became a part of United Air Lines. The M-1 sold to PAT for $2400.00 and the 200 hp J-4B Wright engines added an additional $5000.00. The historic photograph shows an M-1 landing in San Francisco enroute to Los Angeles from Seattle during the first southbound airmail flight of CAM 8. The date was September 15, 1926 and A. W. Starbuck was the pilot.

M-1 (OX-5 90 hp)   Experimental   (1 Modified), 1926

The M-1 was a versatile aircraft and by using a variety of "quick change" engine mounts accepted anything from the 90 hp Curtiss OX-5 to the 200 hp Wright J-4. Shown here is the one M-1 flown with the OX-5 engine. In its original configuration shown here the radiator is located above the fuselage. This was later moved below the fuselage to reduce interference with the airflow over the wing. The OX-5 was tested on the M-1 because there were lots of these surplus engines available and they were relatively inexpensive. In order to get actual flying performance information, the first M-1 was flown with a number of different engines. The OX-5 installation was underpowered and the M-1 (c/n 1) was re-engined and sold with the Hisso 180 hp engine installed.

M-1 (Super Rhone 120 hp)   Experimental   1 built, 1926

Another of the experimental engine installations was the 120 hp Super Rhone engine. However this engine, like the 110 hp LeRhone and the 90 hp OX-5 proved to be not enough for the relatively heavy M-1 and so was never produced. The 150 hp Hisso and 200 hp Wright Whirlwind were the standard engine installations. This close-up shows the engine installation clearly with a good view of the "jeweled" cowling — a trademark of the early Ryan airplanes. Legend has purported that the jeweling was to cover up sloppy workmanship, but none is evident in this photo of an early airplane. The sunburned T. Claude Ryan, decked out in the latest fashion doesn't look like someone satisfied with sloppy work.

M-2   19 built, 1926-1927

Quite similar in appearance to the M-1 series, which saw improvements introduced on each succeeding aircraft as it was built, the M-2 was powered by the same series of engines. The most common was the Wright-Hispano or "Hisso" E-180. Other installations included the Hisso A-150 and E-2 of 200 hp (shown in above photo). Externally the M-2 was identifiable by the addition of fuselage stringers to the otherwise flat sides of the M-1. The M-2 was a rugged and dependable airplane and was operated by a variety of private individuals and companies. One of the M-2's (c/n 22, G-CAJK) was used on skies in Canada and floated out to sea on an ice floe and was lost. Construction/number range was from 11 through 29 with an M-1 and M-3 airframe or two mixed in.

M-2 (Ryan-Siemens 125 hp)   2 built, 1926

In early 1927 T. Claude Ryan arranged for the American distributorship of the German built Siemens-Halske engines. These excellent air-cooled radial engines were shipped to New York where the nameplates were changed to Ryan-Siemens. Ryan was selling more engines than were being delivered and this eventually resulted in the termination of the arrangement. Two of the M-2 airplanes (c/n 24, C-141E) and (c/n 29, 2341) were later powered with this engine. When Ryan sold his half interest in the companies (Ryan Flying Co., Ryan Airlines and Los Angeles-San Diego Airline) he received $25,000 and one of the M-2 airplanes in which he installed the Ryan-Siemens engine.

M-2 (Menasco-Salmson)　　　　　　　　Experimental　　　　　　　　(2 ∓ modified), 1927

At least two of the M-1 and M-2 airplanes were modified to use the Menasco Motors Co. (Los Angeles) modification of the French World War I, Salmson 250 hp water-cooled radial engine. Menasco was converting these to air-cooling and shown above is M-2 (c/n 11, C3253) with this engine installed. One airplane (see story with M-1 Wright-Hispano A-150) which has been held for "evidence" in the trial of a man who had purchased several M-1 airplanes, was returned to Ryan in bad shape. This airplane (possibly M-1, c/n ?, 3122) was rebuilt, sold to Menasco and re-engined with the Salmson modification. These airplanes had no brakes and a tail skid was used for directional stability on the dirt fields. But it made moving them by hand unwieldy so fancy carts were sometimes made — check out that beauty under C3253!

M-3C　　　　　　　　　　　　　　　　　　　　　　　　　　　　　　　　　　1 built, 1927

There was one M-3C (c/n 20, C-10026) built for Howard Hughes to replace an M-2 lost while filming "Hells Angels". The M-3C was owned by Wilson Aero Service of Glendale, California and was used for film work, passenger charter and joyriding until 1933. Power was the 180 hp Hisso V-8 water-cooled engine. In the photo above, note that the cabin enclosure is made by simply adding flat safteeglass to the existing fuselage tubing. Several of the M-1 and M-2 types were field converted with a similar enclosure becoming an M-2C (c/n 16, C-2345 and c/n 26, C-1317) and M-1C (c/n 23, 2532). This latter aircraft is presently the only remaining Ryan "M" airplane and is on display at the San Diego Aerospace Museum.

—Wilson Aero Service via John Underwood

Bluebird   1 built, 1926

M-1 (c/n 10, 3219) the first of the airplanes with an improved "I-beam" wing spar designed by John K. Northrop was later converted into a 5-place closed cabin airplane. This became the one Bluebird, so named because of its color. A "hotter flying" airplane close to the ground, the Bluebird was often flown by T. Claude Ryan. Powered by the 200 hp V-8 Hisso E, built under license by Wright, the plane had the same 36 ft wing of the earlier M-1 and the same flat sided fuselage from the cabin to the rear. However, the pilot now sat in front with room for four passengers and baggage behind him. The Bluebird crashed on landing at Los Angeles when the passenger opened the cabin door to wave and the plane sideslipped into the ground and flipped over. The pilot Doug Kelley and passenger were not injured seriously and the Bluebird was trucked back to San Diego where the remains were used in the construction of an M-2.

B.1 Brougham (Wright J-5)   ATC 25 (Jan 27, 1928)   142 built, 1927-1928

The first B.1 Brougham (c/n 29, 3009) was under construction when all work on it was dropped to concentrate on Lindbergh's special order. In the terribly hectic weeks following Lindbergh's flight, the five-place closed cabin monoplane was completed in time for Frank Hawks to fly it to Washington to welcome Lindbergh on his return from Paris. Basking in the glory of being the "sister" ship to the Spirit of St. Louis, the B.1 was the most widely produced Ryan built by the original company that T. Claude Ryan founded. There were 150 B.1's built (142 Wright J-5, 3 Hisso, 5 special jobs). The 225 hp Wright J-5 powered B.1 sold for $9700.00 and orders were turned away as people clamored for an airplane like the N.Y.P. Shown is (c/n 39, NC3257). The first B.1 with an ATC was c/n 48, NS-15. The last one built was in San Diego and was finished during October 1928.

N.Y.P. (Spirit of St. Louis)

1 built, 1927

A $25,000 prize offered by Raymond Orteig on May 22, 1919 for the first nonstop flight between New York and Paris, and a chance for fame inspired the world's aviation community. The fact that eight years after it was offered it was accomplished by a lone American in a single engine airplane, by a dark horse, an underdog and against better financed and equipped competitors were all ingredients that catapulted Charles A. Lindbergh and his airplane, the Spirit of St. Louis into everlasting fame. Because so much has been written about the flight it is often difficult to separate legend from fact. Three excellent published accounts tell in accurate detail and with feeling, the events of early 1927 as Lindbergh and Ryan Airlines, Inc. (as the company was then called) built and tested the airplane and flew the New York to Paris Flight. These are William Wagner's Chapter 12 of RYAN, THE AVIATOR (McGraw Hill, 1971) and Charles A. Lindbergh's SPIRIT OF ST. LOUIS (Charles Scribner's Sons, 1953) and WE (G. P. Putnam's Sons, 1927).

But, can we separate a few hard facts about the airplane itself? The application for an airplane license from the Department of Commerce, Aeronautics Branch gives us a clue. Charles Lindbergh lettered in "EXPERIMENTAL" above the application title and under "manufacturer's type" lettered in Ryan N.Y.P. The official number as issued on April 27, 1927 was N-X211 and was signed by Wm. P. MacCracken, Jr., assistant secretary of commerce. The Aeronautics Branch nameplate, probably removed after the flight and now in the Missouri Historical Society Library at St. Louis, shows *no* company c/n and Identification Mark N-X211. It is interesting to note that despite all paperwork showing N-X211 the airplane was painted N-X-211.

First inquiries were received from Lindbergh and his St. Louis backers on February 3, 1927. At this time general manager of Ryan Airlines, Inc., T. Claude Ryan was on hand to see that they were properly answered. However Ryan had sold out to B. F. Mahoney the past November but stayed on as general manager until shortly before Lindbergh's departure from San Diego on May 10. Ryan's role certainly must have been one of frustration in seeing his name and company he started, catapulted into international fame as he sat on the sidelines. That he persevered in aviation is a tribute to his personal character.

The go-ahead for building the N.Y.P. was given on February 25, 1927 by Lindbergh personally after consultation with Mahoney, Donald Hall (who had just signed on as the company's only full time engineer) and others of the Ryan organization. There was a 60-day design and delivery time limit and this was met for the N.Y.P. was moved from the Ryan factory to Dutch Flats on April 27. First

flight, the 60th day, was April 28. It is interesting to note that on this first flight Lindbergh and the N.Y.P. engaged a Curtiss Navy Hawk fighter in mock combat.

The airplane was built like an M-2, with a fabric covered steel tubing fuselage and spruce wing spars and ribs. Heart of any airplane is the engine — the N.Y.P. had the finest available, the 223 hp Wright J-5C. Fuel capacity was the main feature, with a total of 450 gallons of fuel on board: 209 in the main fuselage tank, 89 in the nose and 153 in three wing tanks. Oil capacity was 28 gallons. Top speed was 130 mph and the cruising speed was 105. The wing, designed for the Brougham at 42 ft was lengthened to 46 ft without moving the struts outboard. Length was 27 ft 3-in. Gross weight was 4750 lb.

The N.Y.P. was tested from April 28 to May 9 at San Diego. On May 10 they departed for St. Louis, setting a speed record of 14 hours 25 minutes for the 1550 mile flight. On the 12th they flew to New York in 7 hours 20 minutes, setting another record. The flight to Paris was delayed by bad weather until, loaded with 450 gallons of gasoline for the first time, Lindbergh and the Spirit of St. Louis departed for Paris on May 20 at 7:51 A.M. 33 hours and 30 minutes, 3610 miles later at 10:00 P.M. they landed at LeBourget Field at Paris amidst 100,000 screaming people and accomplishing the nonstop flight.

On tour between June 16, 1927 and April 30, 1928, Lindbergh and the N.Y.P. set over 100 unofficial speed and distance records while flying around the USA, Central and South America and the West Indies. The N.Y.P. was placed on permanent exhibit at the National Air Museum at the Smithsonian Institution, Washington, D.C.

NYP-2 1 built, 1927

One exact copy of Lindbergh's NYP was constructed in the summer of 1927. This was the NYP-2 (c/n 36, J-BACC) which was purchased jointly by Tonichi and Damai, abbreviations for newspapers published in Tokyo and Osaka. The all silver NYP-2 was shipped to Japan that summer. An exact copy of the Spirit of St. Louis, even including the large 46 ft wing, the NYP-2 set a new Japanese distance and endurance record by flying 2000 kilometers (1243 miles) in a 13 hour 23 minute dawn to dusk flight on April 28, 1928. Flight was over a circular course over central Japan. Because of bad weather, pilot Fumio Habuto flew most of the time at less than a thousand feet. After the flight Habuto was called the Japanese Lindbergh. Little is known of the plane's use after the record flight, and it was scrapped in 1938.

B.1 Brougham (Hisso) 3 built, 1927

Alternate engines had been the order of the day with the early Ryans, but by the time of the B.1 the engine was standardized with the Wright J-5 of 220 hp. However three Hisso Broughams (c/n 31, C-3007; c/n 46, NC3226 and one not licensed) were built. After ATC 25 was issued (c/n 48 and up) there were no further Hisso powered Broughams built. Sometimes referred to as a B.2 c/n 31 started life with a 150 hp Hisso "A" engine. This was changed to the 180 hp Hisso and in 1928 to the J-4 Wright and in 1929 to the J-5B which was the standard Brougham engine. Photo shows the second Hisso Brougham (c/n 46, NC3226) as the Betty Rogers. It is interesting to note that the B.1's were usually painted: RYAN B.1—MFG BY MAHONEY AIRCRAFT CORP. The third Hisso powered Brougham reportedly got as far as Los Angeles on a delivery flight and developed engine trouble. It was returned to Ryan, re-engined and sold as a Wright J-5 powered B.1.

B.1X ATC 25 (Jan 27, 1928) 1 built, 1928

The B.1X was a special one-of-a-kind job for Charles A. Lindbergh. It was a "factory special" and special attention was given during its construction. B.1X (c/n 69, NX4215) was presented to Lindbergh on April 5, 1929. The engine, a special nickel-plated Wright J-5 and all of the instruments were donated by the various manufacturers — with an eye to publicity. Lindbergh didn't want any publicity but the May 1928 issue of AERO DIGEST proves who won . . . . several of the ads in that issue are presented later in this book. Like the 'Spirit' the B.1X had a 46 foot wingspan with landing lights at the tip of each wing (the regular B.1 had a 42 ft wingspan). Another B.1 with a 46 ft wing was c/n 79, NC4654. Lindbergh used the B.1X for a year or so and then returned it to the builder in good shape. Nothing is known of its later use.

B.1 (MGM Special) 1 built, 1927

One of the most unusual airplanes of all time was the special B.1 version built to accomodate Leo the Lion, the MGM Symbol. This was a B.1 (c/n 42, 1550) and was built by B. F. Mahoney Aircraft Corp and leased to MGM to fly Leo non-stop from San Diego to New York for publicity. Pilot for the plane was Martin Jensen, who placed second in the Dole race to Hawaii. Jensen, with the 450 lb Leo and 400 gallons of gasoline on board departed for New York on September 16, 1927. Unfortunately the engine overheated (high OAT and poor cooling) and they crashed while trying to clear the Mogollon Rim in eastern Arizona. That Jensen and Leo were both rescued is one of the most interesting "believe it or not" stories ever told. The B.1 was a total loss and in fact Mahoney Aircraft had to refund some $2200 or $1 for every mile they landed short of New York.

B.1 Special (Pot Bellied Brougham)   1 Built, 1927

Built for a "Holy City to Holy City" flight (Holy City, California in the Santa Cruz Mountains to Rome, Italy) the Pot Bellied Brougham as it was called never did attempt this honorable flight. Built for Father William Riker and one of his followers, a wealthy widow Mrs. Evelyn Rosencrantz, the B.1 Special (c/n 49, X3598) sported the 46 foot wing of the long-range Broughams. The ill-founded project foundered and the airplane was later sold to Southwest Ryan Airlines of Tulsa, Oklahoma. Once more nothing is known of its use or final disposition. The plane was to have cost 'Father' Riker $20,000. It had been modified to stow the extra fuel beneath the fuselage — giving it the pot bellied appearance and its nickname.

B.3 Brougham   ATC 104 (Jan 24, 1929)   9 built, 1928-1929

The B.3 was a transitionary aircraft between the end of B.1 production in San Diego and start up of the B.5 in St. Louis. Built by Mahoney Aircraft Corporation and the Mahoney-Ryan Aircraft Corp. the 220 hp Wright J-5 powered the six-place B.3. Changes from the B.1 included a wider cabin interior, larger control surfaces, optional dual controls and the ailerons were moved in from the wingtips. Construction number range was 179 to 186 for the B.3. The last four were approved on Mar 26, 1929 under memo 2-50 as a five-place ship with the P&W R-975 of 300 hp. One B.3A (c/n 210, N311K) was built with the B.5 sequence and was approved July 31, 1929 under memo 2-105 with a Wright J-5. Shown is B.3 (c/n 185, C7737) with girl-pilot Marvel Crosson as pilot. Sponsored by Mutual Aircraft Corp, one of the largest Mahoney-Ryan distributors, she set a woman's world altitude record of 23,996 ft in this plane.

B.5 Brougham   ATC 142 (June 13, 1929)   61 built, 1929

Main difference in the B.5 and the early B.3 was the change from the Wright J-5C of 220 hp to the Wright J-6-9 of 300 hp. The first 30 B.5 were produced by Mahoney-Ryan Aircraft Corp and the last 31 were produced by the Ryan Aircraft Corporation (Div. of Detroit Aircraft Corp.). These planes were "Ryan" in name only — they were four steps away from T. Claude Ryan's original company. The B.5 was produced as a six-place landplane and as a six-place seaplane with Edo "Q" floats. There was a single B.5A (c/n 200, NC-15H) approved by memo 2-220 on June 13, 1930 with a P&W Wasp Jr of 300 hp. Many of the B.5 were exported (5 to China, 22 to Mexico and several to Canada). Shown is B.5 (c/n 228, NC728M). Note that the exhaust collector ring has moved to the front of the engine in the B.3 and B.5 airplanes.

B 7 Brougham   ATC 262 (Oct 26, 1929)   8 built, 1929

Aviation was moving fast in the late 1920's, and the vast differences in the M-1 and the B 7 are good examples of this. The basic design had grown from a three-place open cockpit, powered by anything from 90 to 200 hp, to a fully enclosed, six-place cabin plane with 420 hp selling for $19,000. But, the handwriting was on the wall — the Brougham had been stretched about as far as it would go, original company people with vision were long gone and the biggest factor of all — the depression was on hand. Sporting a new paint job, larger tail surfaces, a 420 hp P&W Wasp C1, the B 7 was the ultimate Brougham. Shown here is the first (c/n 249, NC549N) which later went to Mexico as XA-CEO. One B 7, (c/n 255, NC723M) was approved by memo 2-223 June 16, 1930 with a 450 hp Wasp for National Airlines. No B 7's have survived.

C 1 Foursome   ATC 346 (Aug 11, 1930)   3 built, 1930

Looking very much like a scaled down Brougham (which it was), the C 1 was designed to compete in the economic market of the depression. The fact it did not make it is no reflection on a fine airplane — the market just was not there. At the time the C 1 was developed, it was being built by Ryan Aircraft Corporation (Div. of Detroit Aircraft Corp). Other "Divisions" of Detroit were such names as Lockheed, Eastman, Blackburn, Aircraft Development, Marine Aircraft and Winton Aviation Engine. The ATC approval was for a C 1 with the 240 hp Wright R-760 (J-6-7). An approval for an experimental installation of a Packard R-980 diesel was issued to c/n 401. In 1938, the same c/n 401 (NC 557N) started out on a flight from Nova Scotia to Palestine and was never heard from again.

X-1 (90 hp Warner)   Experimental   1 built, 1928

The X-1 Mahoney-Ryan Special or "Doodle Bug" was designed by Donald A. Hall, engineer on the Spirit of St. Louis. Incorporating such advanced ideas as a flying "stabilator" (in use with a different control system in 1975), no "fixed" tail surfaces, and a gearshift control to change the angle of incidence of the stabilator. The ideas were too radical though and perfection was not possible with the 1928 technology. The X-1 (no c/n, X7621) was designed, built and test flown while the B.1 Brougham was entering production and its teething problems were left unsolved. Test pilot Red Harrigan said after his first flight in the X-1 that, "it was completely unrelated to any previous flying experience".

X-1 (110 hp Warner Scarab)　　　　　　　　　　Experimental　　　　　　　　　　(1 modified), 1929

Even though the X-1 was not proving to be the "airplane of the future" experiments continued with it. Built and first flown in San Diego in September 1928, it was later shipped to St. Louis where the Mahoney factory had moved. With $50,000 invested in the project and perfection still not attained, Mahoney finally dropped the X-1. Don Hall spent the next several years in an independent attempt at perfecting his ideas but was not successful. The X-1, with a 7-cylinder air cooled radial 110 hp Warner Scarab installed, was flown by Lindbergh several times.

CM-1 (Ryan Mechanics Monoplane Co.)　　　　　　　　　　1 built, 1928

The CM-1 (Cantilever, Monoplane) was built by an organization of former Ryan employees who remained in California when the original company moved to St. Louis. The new design was not related to T. Claude Ryan who was understandably sensitive about the continued use of his name in projects with which he was not concerned, so Ryan Mechanics (Los Angeles) changed their name to Federal Aircraft Corporation (San Bernardino, Calif). Their CM-1 (NX4041), designed to carry six was named the Lone Eagle and flew Feb 12, 1928. It featured a 37 ft 6-in. fully cantilever wing of tubular steel construction — including the spars and ribs. Engine was the 200 hp Wright J-4B. Later a 260 hp Menasco Salmson was substituted. The company built several airplanes, the CM-1, a CM-2 (6 place, strut braced wing, Wasp engine) and a CM-3 (X7667). The undercapitalized company suspended operations in mid-1929.

S-T "Sport-Trainer"　　　　　　　　　　ATC 541 (June 21, 1934)　　　　　　　　　　5 built, 1934-1937

In late 1933 and early 1934, T. Claude Ryan designed what would eventually prove to be one of the most sought after classic airplanes of all time — the Ryan S-T — the Sport-Trainer. The first S-T (c/n 101, X14223) flew on June 8, 1934 with John A. Fornasero at the controls. Just two weeks later on June 21, after company and CAA tests, ATC 541 was issued to The Ryan Aeronautical Co. for the S-T. Powered with the 95 hp four-cylinder inline, aircooled, inverted Menasco B4 engine, the S-T was a two-place tandem, open cockpit fully monocoque fuselage airplane with aluminum ribs, spruce spars and fabric covered flying surfaces. The first S-T airplanes sold for $3985. Only five (c/n 101, 102, 104, 117 and 155) were built as most preferred the 125 hp STA. The first S-T crashed Dec 19, 1934 and only one (c/n 117) remains.

STA　　　　　　　　　　ATC 571 (May 23, 1935)　　　　　　　　　　71 built, 1935-1940

Change to the 125 hp Menasco C4 Pirate engine resulted in the peppier STA. Externally similar to the S-T, all of the STA airplanes had the STA-1 airframe; characterized by "small" cockpit openings, internal fuselage longerons, a low swept back windshield, non-adjustable seats, heel brakes and no-turnover post. Two STA (c/n 312 and 355) were originally produced with a larger cockpit (like the YPT-16) and had dual flap controls, however by 1975 these modifications have been made to many of the early airplanes. Most common of the civilian "S-T" series, an unmodified STA is considered the "classic" version. There were six STA built in 1935, 26 (selling for $4685) in 1936 and 34 (selling for $4585) in 1937. Shown is c/n 128, NC16039 in which Tex Rankin won the 1937 International Aerobatic championship in St. Louis. STA top speed was 150 mph and cruise was 127, range 350 miles.

STA-Special　　　　　　　　　　　　　　　　　　ATC 681　　　　　　　　　　　　　　　　　　11 built, 1936-1939

Addition of the 150 hp Menasco C 4S supercharged Super Pirate gave the STA-Special a top speed of 160 mph at sea level and a cruise of 135 at 2000 ft. Shown is STA-Special (c/n 180, NACA-96) which was delivered to the National Advisory Committee for Aeronautics on August 2, 1938 because, "the STA-Special is the only plane of its size which has transport plane operation characteristics". Externally similar to the STA, the STA-Special was an STA-1 airframe identifiable by an oil radiator beneath the cowling and no air inlet hole in the left side of the nose. Price new in 1937 was $5185. Later export STA-Specials (STM) were added to the ATC 681. In 1975 only two original STA-Specials remain, c/n 188 and 339. The Special carried 24 gal. of gas, 3 of oil and had a gross weight of 1575 lb, useful load 529 and empty weight of 1046 lb.

STB　　　1 built, 1935

Built in 1935 as a single seater with no front seat or cockpit, there was one STB. In place of the front seat was a special long range fuel tank. The STB was built on special order for sportsman Cliff Durant. The STB (c/n 109, NC14953) was powered by the Menasco C4 engine of 125 hp, and was delivered Nov 6, 1935. On Jan 27, 1938, the STB was converted to STA configuration and in 1939 was destroyed in an accident at Sacramento, California. The STB had the same external dimensions as the rest of the S-T series airplanes — length 21 ft 5-3/8-in., height 6 ft 11-in. and wingspan of 29 ft 11-in. Idea was similar to later Chinese STM-2P.

STM (STA-Special)　　　　　　　　　　ATC 681 — Light Fighter　　　　　　　　　　22 built, 1937-1938

Advertised is a "light fighter" or trainer, the STA-Special was sold to several South and Central American countries as an STM — the "M" for Military. Powered with the 150 hp C4S Menasco engine for operation at higher field elevations, these airplanes were identical to the STA-Special and were built under the same ATC. Some like the Guatemalan STM above, had machine guns mounted on the top of each wing. Others had a gun mounted in front of the rear cockpit like a WWI fighter. These STM's were an STA-1 airframe. Deliveries included six for Mexico, three for Honduras, 12 for Guatemala and one for Ecuador. Two additional STA-Specials were sent to South America — c/n 141 to Nicaragua and c/n 199 to Bolivia. By 1975, seven of the Guatemalan airplanes and one Mexican STM had been returned to the USA.

XPT-16　　　　　　　　　　Air Corps Trainer　　　　　　　　　　1 built, 1939

Following a competition at Wright Field in early 1939, Ryan was awarded a contract for one XPT-16 (c/n 306, ex-NC-18907, AAC s/n 39-717) on June 8. The low wing monoplane XPT-16 was the first break with the military's "biplane trainer" tradition, and paved the way for almost 1500 Ryan trainers in World War II. First flight of the XPT-16 was on Feb 3, 1939 and it was delivered to the USAAC on June 6. It was powered with the Menasco C-4 (c/n 425) engine of 125 hp (military designation L-365-1). On Jan 1, 1941, the XPT-16 became the XPT-16A with installation of the Kinner B-5 radial of 125 hp (military designation R-440-1). The one XPT-16 was used operationally along with the YPT-16 and PT-20 airplanes at the Ryan schools training military (not civilian or CPT) pilots. On July 12, 1941 it was surveyed "Class 26" with 1023 hours.

YPT-16   Air Corps trainer   15 built, 1939

The Air Corps defined the YPT-16 as a two-place, low wing, wire braced monoplane with one additional reinforcing strut on each side of the fuselage. Although it did have the larger cockpit cutouts and a turnover post, it was still considered an STA-1 airframe. The YPT-16 (and XPT-16) differed from commercial STA versions by having a steerable and full swiveling tail wheel, larger cockpits, dual Army instrumentation and wing tie down and towing lugs. The YPT-16 had an engine starter. Powered with the Menasco C-4 of 125 hp at 2175 rpm. the YPT-16 had a top speed of 128 mph and a service ceiling of 15,000 ft. Two YPT-16 were delivered in July 1939, the other 13 in August, C/n range was 307-321 plus 338. C/n 315 was the high time Air Corps YPT-16 trainer with 1291 hours when removed from service. None survive in 1975.

YPT-16A/XPT-16A   Air Corps trainer   (14 modified), 1941

As World War II loomed closer, the Air Corps accelerated its training effort. The Ryan trainers were worked hard and there was some complaint that the Menasco engines were not holding up under the hard usage of pilot training. Several engine installations were experimented with (STW, STK) but the final decision was substitution of a five-cylinder 125 hp Kinner B-5 (R-440-1) radial engine for the inline Menasco. Thirteen YPT-16 and the one XPT-16 became the YPT-16A and XPT-16A. Additionally, the wheel skirts and fairings were often removed. A hand crank was installed on the left side of the airplane. No YPT-16 aircraft survive in 1975. C/n 319 and 338 were wrecked before the modification program started and were never YPT-16A.

PT-20 Air Corps trainer 30 built, 1939-1940

Operational experience with the YPT-16 led to orders for 30 PT-20 (c/n 323-337, 340-354) with changes resulting in the first STA-2 airframes. Primary difference was further increase in cockpit size by movement of fuselage longeron from the inside of the cockpit to the outside of the fuselage. Otherwise the airplanes were identical and were used interchangably with the YPT-16 at the Ryan schools training Dodos (new cadets) for the Air Corps. Powered by the C-4 (military L-365-1) Menasco of 125 hp three PT-20 were converted to PT-20B (c/n 324, 332 and one other) with installation of the D-4 engine. Photo shows last PT-20 built (c/n 354, 40-2416) which was delivered to Wright Field April 9, 1940 and surveyed "Class 26" in 1943 with only 298 hours. Air Force contract AC-15566 specification R-703-10 called for 773 PT-20 airplanes — none of which were built!

PT-20A Air Corps trainer (27 modified), 1940-1941

Change to the five-cylinder radial Kinner (R-440-1) B-5 125 hp engine from the four-cylinder inline, inverted Menasco engines resulted in the PT-20A. Twenty-seven of the 30 PT-20 airplanes were modified, and all were used interchangably at the Ryan schools. Not converted was c/n 342 and two others, c/n unknown. First PT-20 (c/n 323, AAC s/n 40-3387) was delivered Dec 12, 1939, the remainder in 1940. Conversion to PT-20A configuration started in October 1940. High time PT-20A was c/n 329 with 1342 hours. Known surplus sales were c/n 325 and 352 (N69094 survives in 1975). Price of the original PT-20 version was $6380. These airplanes retained the good flying characteristics of the STA series, but wheel pants and other refinements were often removed in military service.

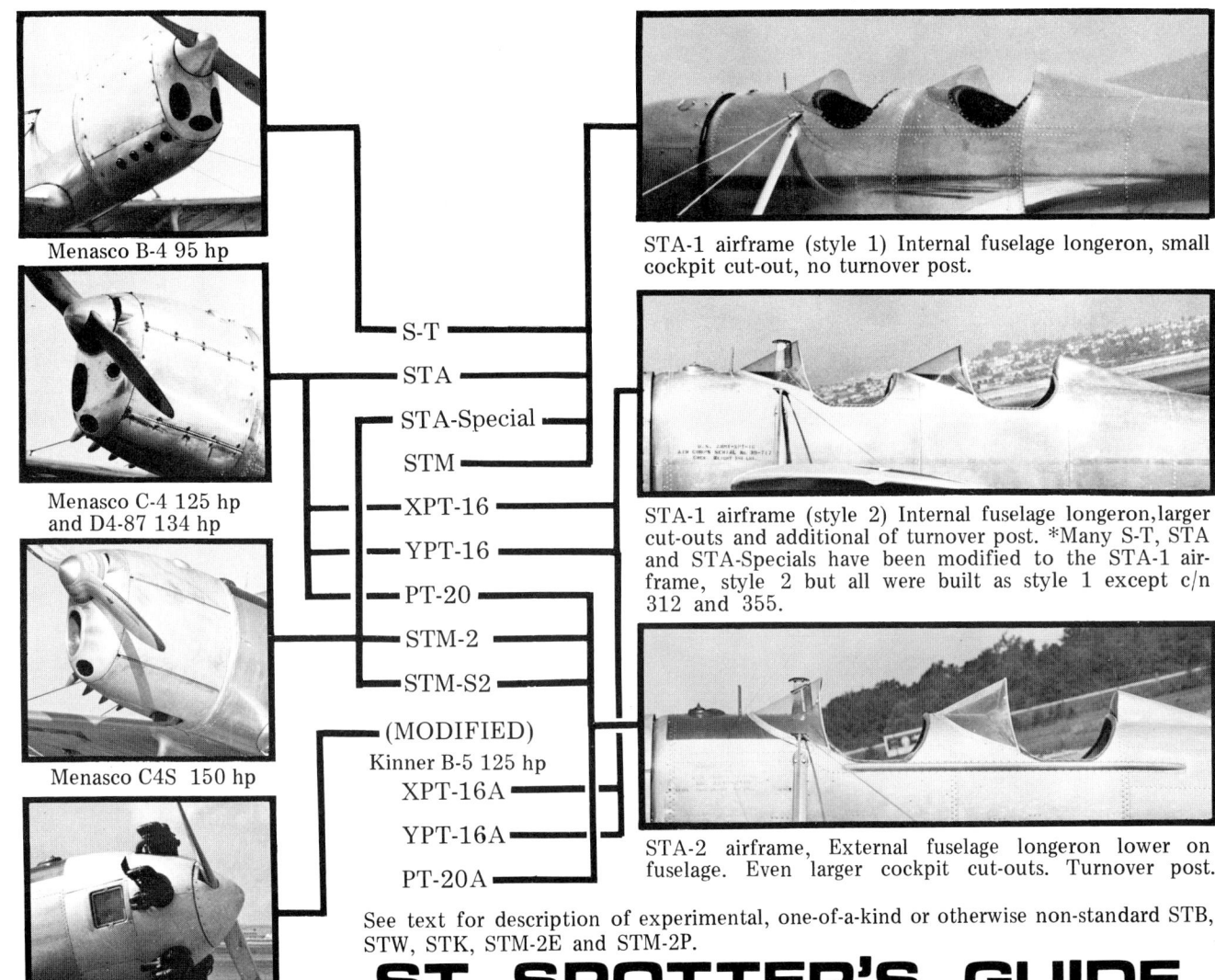

STK   Experimental   1 built, 1941

There was one experimental STK (c/n 406, NX18924) built, and it remains as something of a mystery in the Ryan history. The experimental license on file with the FAA states that STK, c/n 406, is to "determine engine suitability". Photo shows the STK with the 125 hp Kinner B-5 installed. This is the engine used to convert the YPT-16 and PT-20 into the "A" models and it makes sense that this is the prototype for the Kinner conversion. It is an STA-2 airframe of the PT-20 (in fact PT-20 style stenciling is visible on the landing gear cover and fuselage), but it is also the only STA series airplane to sport the three-piece windshield of the later ST-3 airplanes. So what became of it after the engine trials? Was it modified to production configuration, given a different c/n and delivered as an STM-2 or –S2? Did it crash? Was it scrapped? Maybe time will clear up this mystery.

Menasco B-4 95 hp

Menasco C-4 125 hp and D4-87 134 hp

Menasco C4S 150 hp

S-T
STA
STA-Special
STM
XPT-16
YPT-16
PT-20
STM-2
STM-S2
(MODIFIED)
Kinner B-5 125 hp
XPT-16A
YPT-16A
PT-20A

STA-1 airframe (style 1) Internal fuselage longeron, small cockpit cut-out, no turnover post.

STA-1 airframe (style 2) Internal fuselage longeron, larger cut-outs and additional of turnover post. *Many S-T, STA and STA-Specials have been modified to the STA-1 airframe, style 2 but all were built as style 1 except c/n 312 and 355.

STA-2 airframe, External fuselage longeron lower on fuselage. Even larger cockpit cut-outs. Turnover post.

See text for description of experimental, one-of-a-kind or otherwise non-standard STB, STW, STK, STM-2E and STM-2P.

ST SPOTTER'S GUIDE

STW   Experimental   (2 modified) 1939

There were two STW airplanes used to test the suitability of Warner engines on the STA airframe. STW (c/n 338, NX18919) was issued its license on May 29, 1939 with a Warner SCA-50 Scarab engine of 160 hp (derated to 2050 rpm and 145 hp by a throttle stop). The second STW (c/n 337, NX18920) was licensed June 21, 1939 with the 125 hp Warner installed. After tests with the Warner engine, the standard Menasco C 4 engines were re-installed. C/n 337 became PT-20 40-2401 and shown below as an STW, c/n 338 became YPT-16 40-53.

STM-2E and STM-2P   Chinese trainer and fighter   50 built, 1940

Operational photo of a "Chinese" STM-2E trainer, published for the first time, was taken by AVG pilot at Kunming. Wheel fairings are removed and camouflage dabbled on. Aircraft No. 42 shown is possibly c/n 397 and listed as No. 42R. On November 15, 1939, Ryan signed a contract for 48 STM-2E two-place primary trainers (c/n 356-374, 377-405) and two single-place pursuit trainers (c/n 375, 376). The two STM-2P pursuit trainers (see photo lower right, page 120) each had one 30-caliber fixed machine gun installed inside the fuselage and the forward cockpit sealed. These airplanes had the same STA-2 airframe of the PT-20, but with the C4S-2 engine of 165 hp. These 50 airplanes representing 15.8 percent of all ST series production were shipped to China where like so many things, their individual histories are no longer traceable. All however, were destroyed or captured by the Japanese and later destroyed. Official designation is STM-2E, also referred to as: STM-E2, STC-4 and ST-C5. The pursuit trainer is officially STM-2P, also known as: STM-P2, STC-P4 and STC-P5.

STM-2   ATC 681 — Dutch trainer (Army)   108 built, 1940-1941

There were a total of 108 STM-2 and STM-S2 trainers built for the Dutch. These airplanes were delivered in 1940 and 1941 to Java (Netherlands East Indies) and were the STA-2 airframe of the PT-20 and the 150 hp supercharged C 4S engine of the STA-Special. They were built under ATC 681. The Netherlands East Indies Air Arm (Army) operated 60 landplanes from Bandoeng. These were c/n's 407-446, 495-514. All were lost to Japanese action or were captured. No STM-2 aircraft survived the war. A special chapter on the epic story of these airplanes is on page 90 of this book. The first 12 airplanes for the Dutch were shipped from Los Angeles on Nov 18, 1940 on the SS Hoegh Silver Dawn. An additional eight left on Dec 7, 1940 on the MS Java and the others in the order were all shipped by early 1941.

STM-S2   ATC 681 — Dutch trainer (Navy)   Total built included with STM-2

The Dutch Navy STM-S2 (c/n 447-494) airplanes lived an exciting life — from military trainer on wheels or floats, to scout and warplane, from the USA to Java, to Australia and back to the USA. They were shipped to Morokrembangan Naval Air Base, Java just before World War II. During Japanese attacks on Java, the 48 STM-S2 operated by the Dutch Naval Air Service were pressed into use as scouts, liaison and harbor patrol aircraft, often flying from flooded rice paddies. Thirty-four STM-S2 were evacuated from Java on Feb 17, 1942 and were used briefly by the Dutch in Australia, then were turned over to the Royal Australian Air Force. Twenty-six of these survived the war and in 1946 were sold surplus by the RAAF. By 1975, six of these had been destroyed, six returned to the USA, 12 flying in Australia, one is in a trade school and one in a museum in New Zealand. Identical to the STM-2 except for a larger front spar in the stub wing, the STM-S2 were built under ATC 681 and are licensable as "normal category" aircraft in the USA. 84 STM-2 and 24 STM-S2 were ordered, however most if not all of the 48 Navy aircraft were delivered as STM-S2. Shown is c/n 447.

ST-3 (basic configuration) (ST-3KB)

The ST-3 (c/n 1000, NX18925) first flight was on October 9, 1940 and it was powered by a Kinner B-54 engine rated at 125 hp at 1975 rpm. Compression ratio is 5.5:1 with this engine. Proposed at this time (but never built) was a ST-3M, powered by either the Menasco D4 of 125 hp or C4S of 150 hp at 3000 ft.

ST-3   Experimental   2 built, 1940

Incorporating changes brought about as a result of military operations, two prototype ST-3 airplanes were built. These were the forerunners of the PT-21, NR-1 and PT-22 airplanes described later. First flight of the ST-3 (c/n 1000, NX18925) was on Oct 9, 1940 This airplane remained as an experimental company "hack" on which were tried many ideas.

The second ST-3 (c/n 1001, NX18926) was brought up to production standards as an ST-3KR and ATC 749 was issued Feb 16, 1942 for ST-3KR c/n 1001 and up, including PT-22 and PT-22A models. Never a military airplane, this second ST-3 officially became an ST-3KR and is still flying in 1975.

The ST-3 (c/n 1000) was built and first flown with the Kinner B-5 or B-54 engine of 125 hp at 1925 rpm. This was the ST-3KB (Kinner, B engine) occasionally referred to. The photo above shows it in its initial configuration as an ST-3KB.

Although ST-3 was a direct descendent of the STA series airplanes, it was nevertheless a new design. Many changes were apparent including a fuselage 14-in. longer and 3-in wider. "Army" seats with room for a parachute were installed as was a three section windshield. The wheel skirts and fairings were removed and a metal fairing installed. Several fairings were tried out before decision was made to remove them completely. Wheel tread was wider by 12-in. and the wheels were moved further forward. Wings were swept back 4° 10'. A baggage compartment was installed in the left side, back of the rear cockpit. Rudder design was changed to include the tail cone fairing as an integral part of the tail surface.

ST-3 (ST-3KR) ATC 749

The second prototype ST-3 (c/n 1001, NX18926), configured as a PT-22 is shown here at Wright Field for Air Corps tests. At this point, with the Kinner R-55 engine of 160 hp installed it is officially an ST-3KR. It is being tested as a PT-21, and close inspection of the photograph shows it is stenciled PT-22! It is flying in 1975 as a ST-3KR with a Kinner R-56 engine.

ST-3 (Canadian enclosure)

ST-3 (c/n 1000, NX18925) is shown here as modified with a winter enclosure as proposed for the Canadians. This is a particularly handsome enclosure installation considering its 1941 vintage. This version was never produced and the canopy was removed. Subsequent versions show a line of rivets across the back of the fuselage and indicate a rough sequence for the modifications.

ST-3 (Speedring)

Once more the 1st ST-3 (c/n 1000, NX18925) was modified, flying now with the Kinner R-55 engine and a speed ring. Speed was not a factor in the training role, and possible cooling benefits were minimal so the ring was removed from production versions.

ST-3 (ST-3S configuration)

There were three ST-3S airplanes delivered (c/n 1078-1080, AF s/n 41-15174-15176). These went to Ecuador on a lend lease program. One of the most publicized versions the ST-3S got a lot of attention by the press. Shown is the old standby, ST-3 (c/n 1000, NX18925) on twin Edo floats. The Dutch ordered 25 of these with the Menasco engine but they were delivered as a PT-22A with wheels.

ST-3 (Lycoming engine configuration)

ST-3 (c/n 1000, NX18925) was a handy tool for the engineers. Here it is with PT-22 landing gear and the Lycoming 0-435 engine installation as later used in the YPT-25.

PT-21   ATC 749 — Air Corps trainer   100 built, 1941

There were 100 PT-21 (c/n 1002-1059, 1061-1076, 1155-1180) airplanes built by Ryan and all were used by the contract schools training Air Corps pilots. Initially powered by the five-cylinder Kinner R-440-3 of 132 hp, the PT-21 airplanes were converted to PT-22 configuration by removing the landing gear fairings and changing to the Kinner R-540-1 (civil R-55) of 160 hp. This made the PT-21 a PT-22 and the nameplates were stamped over indicating this fact. The PT-21 had tandem open cockpits with complete dual controls and duplicated instruments in both cockpits. Air Corps contract AC-15566 Specification R-703-8 had called for 773 PT-20 airplanes. This was modified to Specification R-703-10 and there were 775 airplanes delivered as 100 PT-21, 100 NR-1 and the first 575 PT-22.

NR-1   ATC 749 — Navy trainer   100 built, 1941

Built concurrently with the PT-21, the NR-1 was the Navy version. There were 100 NR-1 (c/n 1060, 1081-1154, 1181-1205) built and they were identical to the PT-21 except for a lockable tail wheel and the engine was called an L-440-3 Kinner of 132 hp. Shown is the next-to-last NR-1 built (c/n 1204, BuAer 4197). of the 100 NR-1 built, 99 were operated by the Navy at Jacksonville Naval Air Station and one (c/n 1200, BuAer 4193) was used by the Kopper's Co. in Lancaster, Pa. At least three NR-1 (c/n 1129 N66622, c/n 1200 N31687 and one other as N67640) were known sold surplus. The NR-1 had an unpainted fuselage with Navy yellow wings and tail surfaces. Typical of the ST-3 series airplanes, there was a wing walk on both wings. Note that the aileron balance on the NR-1 and PT-21 airplanes is beneath the wing — it is above the wing in the PT-22.

PT-22 Recruit (PT-22C) ATC 749 — Air Corps trainer 1023 built (250 modified), 1941-1942

Ultimate refinement of the military production Ryan trainer was the classic PT-22. Lack of any fragile landing gear covering gave the PT-22 its ungainly bird-legged appearance but made maintenance easier in the rugged use of the military contract schools. Sold new for $8473, 1023 PT-22 were delivered with the Kinner R-55 (military R-540-1) engine of 160 hp at 1850 rpm. Externally identical, 250 became the PT-22C when they were field modified with the slightly different Kinner R-56 (military R-540-3) engine. There was no PT-22B built. Aileron balances were on top of the wing on all PT-22 versions (except modified PT-21). Three lend-lease PT-22 (as ST-3S) went to Ecuador, 70 started to China but were shortstopped in India. Rivaling the more widely produced Stearman Kaydet in popularity, the PT-22 were sold surplus before VJ Day and several hundred survive and operate successfully in 1975.

PT-22A Dutch/U. S. Air Corps trainer 25 built, 1942

Starting life as an ST-3S floatplane trainer for the Dutch Naval Air Services (MLD) the 25 PT-22A were built and delivered as landplane trainers for the U. S. Army Air Corps and used right alongside the other PT-22 versions in contract school inventory. Contract for the ST-3 was signed by the Netherlands Purchasing Commission, May 26, 1941 and called for 25 airplanes powered with the 160 hp Menasco D-4B engines. These airplanes were never built. The contract was amended Jan 8, 1942 to call for 25 ST-3S floatplanes powered by the Kinner R-55 radial. These airplanes were built, but delivered with wheels instead of floats and to the U. S. Air Corps instead of the Dutch Navy. These were c/n 1775-1799. Shown above is what is possibly the only Dutch marked airplane, R-070.

YPT-25 (ST-4) Experimental Air Corps trainer 5 built, 1942

Built to Air Corps contract AC-21204 Specification 714-2 which called for minimum use of "strategic" materials, the YPT-25 (ST-4) was the last of the ST series airplanes built by Ryan. The YPT-25 (AF s/n 42-8703/42-8707) was powered by the 185 hp opposed Lycoming 0-435-1 and was built almost completely of plastic-bonded wood. Other than the engine and cowling, only the landing gear was of metal. The two-place tendem cockpit YPT-25 was the first of the Ryans capable of a front-seat solo — desirable in military flying. The YPT-25 was also equipped for night and "blind" flying. The five airplanes were test flown at Ryan and flown off by WASP pilots. YPT-25 (s/n 42-8703) was surveyed at Salina, Kansas on Sept 2, 1943 and (s/n 42-8705) surveyed at Cimmarron Field, Sept 13, 1944. Performance for the YPT-25 included a top speed of 149 mph, cruise of 134 at 75 percent power.

S-C ATC 651 1 built, 1937

The first S-C (c/n 201, NX17372), Ryan's three-place cabin airplane was a revolutionary product in early 1937. At a time when the civilian airplanes were either "big" like the Gullwing Stinsons, or "little" like the Piper Cub and almost always fabric, the S-C attracted a lot of attention. In typical Ryan fashion construction techniques were ahead of the state of the art and all assemblies were jigged and engineered for mass production. ATC 651 was issued in the summer of 1937. The S-C featured a 43-in. wide front seat with dual stick controls and dual brakes. The rear-seat was 40-in wide, and the sliding cabin hatch could be opened in flight. The S-C served as both S-C and SCW prototype and was delivered in 1938 as an SCW. It operated in Mexico as XA-CUT; by 1975 it was being rebuilt as SCW NC17372.

SCW (prototype)　　　　　　　　　　　ATC 658 (October 1937)　　　　　　　　　　(1 modified), 1937

Following an extensive operational test program by the Ryan Aeronautical Company and at the Ryan School of Aeronautics, decision was made to switch from the supercharged Menasco C 4S to the Warner Super-Scarab radial of 145 hp which was easier to maintain, had greater service life and was less expensive to install. After flight tests with the new engine, ATC 658 was issued to the prototype S-C which had become SCW (c/n 201, NC17372), shown in its final configuration. C/n 201 is the only SCW to have the four-piece front windshield — production airplanes have a two-piece windshield and a beefed-up sliding hatch. Advertised as "all metal" construction, the SCW was actually a composite airplane with half the wing and the empenage being fabric covered. Performance figures are for SCW and (S-C): Top speed 150 mph (152); cruise 135 (136); range 500 miles (520).

SCW (production)　　　　　　　　　　　ATC 658　　　　　　　　　　13 built, 1938-1939

There were a total of 14 SCW airframes built. This includes the prototype (c/n 201) 11 production airplanes (c/n 202-212) and two incomplete airframes (c/n 213, 214). C/n 213 was never finished, but 214 was completed following World War II. Shown above is c/n 204, NC18911. Ryan ordered parts for 25 SCW airplanes but just as production started, large, urgent military orders (STM, YPT-16 and PT-20) were received and production of the SCW was terminated. Base price of the SCW was $6885. SCW sported a distinctive "dive brake" perforated flap located beneath the fuselage just back of the landing gear. Although most have been re-engined with the 165 or 185 hp Warner engines by 1976, 10 of the SCW remain in existence. In 1943 one SCW (c/n 211) was impressed by the Army Air Corps as an L-10 (AF s/n 42-10742) and was sold surplus in 1944. Several SCW served with Civil Air Patrol and were modified to carry bombs.

YO-51 "Dragonfly" (Ryan Model OSR-1)   Experimental STOL   3 built, 1940

Ryan's first venture in STOL airplanes was the imaginatively named YO-51 "Dragonfly" for the Army Air Corps. Built to specification C-413-3A on Air Corps Contract AC-13101, the Dragonfly was built for rough, short field operation as an infantry and artillery support and reconnaissance aircraft. Powered by the Pratt & Whitney R-985-21 Wasp Junior of 420 hp, the YO-51 could clear a 50 ft obstacle in 350 ft and fly as slowly as 32 mph. The 52 ft span, high wing had full span leading edge slots and Fowler flaps along the trailing edge. Ailerons also worked as flaps. The first YO-51 (AC s/n 40-703) was delivered on March 5, 1940 to Wright Field. It was surveyed "Class 26" (training school use) at Sheppard AFB, Wichita Falls, Texas on October 25, 1941 with 325 hours and "fair wear and tear." Delivered in late July 1940, YO-51 (AC s/n 40-704) had 252 hours when placed in "Class 26" in 1941. The third YO-51 (AC s/n 40-705) had 341 hours. The two-place tandem cockpit YO-51 had a 4206 lb gross weight and a top speed of 130 mph. Less expensive, modified "lightplanes" were pressed into military service instead of using these specially designed aircraft like the YO-51. Top photo on roll-out shows the first YO-51 (s/n 40-703) which initially featured circular plates on the elevators, and landing gear struts before fairings were installed. Shown below is YO-51 (s/n 40-703) in its final configuration. OSR stood for Observation Short Range.

XFR-1 "Fireball" (Model 28)   Experimental Navy Fighter   3 built, 1944

With the advent of the jet age the Navy was faced with the problem of getting aircraft which could operate off the carrier deck and take a wave-off since the first jet engines did not provide the "quick" response necessary for these maneuvers. One solution was Ryan's Fireball, a composite aircraft powered by two engines: out front a Wright R-1820-72W nine-cylinder air cooled radial of 1350 hp turning a variable pitch propeller and inside, a General Electric I-16 (later designated J-31) jet of 1600 lb static thrust. The Fireball has the distinction of being Ryan's only multi-engine aircraft built! The prototype XFR-1 (BuAer 48232) flew for the first time June 25, 1944. The second (BuAer 48233) flew on Sept 20, 1944 and the third (BuAer 48234) in October. Major teething problem of the XFR-1 were the tail surfaces which had to be revised. Shown above is the original configuration of the first XFR-1.

FR-1 "Fireball" (Model 28)   Navy fighter   64 built, 1945

An "elite" Navy Squadron (VF-66, Firebirds) with Navy ace Lt. Cdr. John F. Gray as Commanding Officer, was commissioned Jan 1, 1945 and carrier qualifications were carried out in early May aboard the USS Ranger. The Fireball (BuAer 39647/39712) had a top speed of 425 mph at 18,000 ft and with piston engine alone, 320 mph at sea level. Climb to 20,000 ft took 5.6 minutes. However, the FR-1 did not get into combat and with the end of the war orders for 634 were cancelled. The Fireball provided much operational data which aided in future jet design, and a number of "firsts" for the Navy were recorded including: first tricycle landing gear aircraft carrier qualified, first "composite" aircraft with two different types of engine; first full feathering, reversable prop and first flush riveted aircraft. First jet landing was made when the R-1820 quit. Last carrier duty was aboard the USS Rendova in 1947.

XFR-4 "Fireball" (Model 28-5)   Experimental fighter   1 built, 1945

It has been generally accepted that there were 66 FR-1 airplanes built. However, before completion, two FR-1 airframes were modified. One of these became the XFR-4 (BuAer 39665) which had a top speed nearly 100 mph greater than the standard FR-1. This had a Westinghouse J-34 engine of 3400 lb static thrust installed, giving it a top speed in excess of 500 mph. The wing root jet intakes were removed to the sides of the fuselage, further cleaning up the design. At 32 ft 8¾-in, XFR-4 was 8-in. longer than the FR-1. Wingspan was the same at 40 ft. The vertical tail was further modified. Two other experimental models, the XFR-2 and XFR-3 were never built.

XF2R-1 "Dark Shark" (Model 29)   Experimental fighter   1 built, 1946

The second FR-1 airframe removed from the production line was (BuAer 39661). This became the all jet XF2R-1 "Dark Shark" which had the 1700 hp, 550 lb static thrust, General Electric XT31-GE-2 turboprop (also known as TG-100) driving an 11 ft diameter Hamilton Standard prop. Use of this fully reversing (in flight) prop could have given the Dark Shark carrier landing capability without an arresting hook. The XF2R-1 also had the J31-GE-2 Jet engine (1600 lb static thrust) in the fuselage. Without arresting gear, operational radio, folding wings and catapult gear installed, the XF2R-1 had a gross weight of 11,000 lb (compared to the FR-1's 9862 lb). In November 1946 the Dark Shark became the Navy's first turboprop to reach flight testing status. It had a service ceiling of 39,100 ft, an initial rate of climb of 5000 fpm and was 36 ft long.

Navion A (205 Utility and DeLuxe)   ATC 782 (Jan 28, 1947)   1238 built by Ryan, 1947-1951

North American Aviation built the NAvion as a little brother to the P-51 Mustang of World War II fame. They built 1109 NAvions and L-17A's (c/n range NAV-4-2/NAV-4-1110) characterized by a Continental E-185-3 of 185 hp. Between 1947 when Ryan acquired the production rights and 1951 when production terminated due to commitments for the Korean War, Ryan built an additional 1238 airplanes (NAvion, Navion A and B, L-17B and L-17C conversions). C/n range for Ryan built airplanes was NAV-4-1111/NAV-4-2350B. The Navion A (c/n NAV-4-1566 and NAV-4-1628 and higher) was the first Ryan change and was approved on Feb 3, 1949. These models had the Continental E-185-3 or -9 rated at 205 hp and a changed fuel system. The Navion A, advertised in 1950 at $9485, was sold in two versions, the Utility 205 (a stripped, workhorse airplane) and the De Luxe 205 with more comfortable appointments.

Navion B (Super 260)   ATC 782   Total unknown, mixed with standard Navion, 1950-1951

In 1950, Ryan added the Utility 205 (Model A, as was the De Luxe 205) and the Navion Super 260 (Model B) to their line. The Super 260 was approved on March 13, 1950 as a four-place sliding canopy cabin monoplane. Engine was the Lycoming GO-435-C2 of 260 hp at 3400 rpm. Performance was: Model B (Model A); 174 mph maximum speed (163 mph); cruise at 7000 ft, 170 mph (5000 ft and 155 mph); range 415 miles (500 miles); service ceiling 18,000 ft (15,600 ft). Dimensions were identical for all Navion models, wingspan 33 ft 5-in.; length 27 ft 6-in.; height 8 ft 8-in. Gross weight was 2850 lb. After termination of Ryan production in 1951, the popular Navion (shown is NAV-4-2158B) attracted a dedicated following with production continuing through a number of different versions by different companies. The American Navion Society, Box 1175, Banning, CA offers parts and manuals in 1975.

L-17B Navion (L-17C) Army liaison 163 built, 1948-1949

In 1948 Ryan received a contract for 163 L-17B airplanes, which except for avionics were identical to the civilian Navion A. Powered by the 205 hp Continental E-185-3 engine, the L-17B was a four place Army liaison aircraft. It saw extensive use in Korea, being among other things General Douglas MacArthur's personal liaison aircraft. One was even landed on a Navy carrier. North American had produced the L-17A and when modified by Ryan it became the L-17C. A number of the military L-17 were sold surplus following the Korean War.

Model 72 Navy trainer 1 built, 1953

Ryan records show deliveries of 1238 Navion type airplanes. However there were c/n's issued to 1240 airplanes — leaving two unaccounted. One of these is the Model 72. This was a modification of the basic Navion as a Navy trainer which was evaluated at Pensacola in trials held during 1953-1954. Apparent reason for rejection was Navy preference for tandem seating. The modified fully aerobatic Navion was rated to 6G load limit. It had a new wingtip design which increased wingspan by four feet to 37 ft 8-in. Cockpit was converted from a four to two place and a bubble canopy installed. Other modifications included removal of the steering wheel, installation of a control "stick", removal of the aileron/rudder interconnection, toe brakes instead of hand brakes and a free swiveling nose wheel. Engine was the Lycoming GO-435-C2B driving a constant speed rpop.

VZ-3RY — Configuration 1 "Vertiplane"

The experimental vertical take-off and landing VZ-3RY (AR s/n 56-6941) was built for the U. S. Army under the technical direction of the Office of Naval Research. Driven by a single Lycoming T-53-L-1 turbine of 1000 shp, the VZ-3RY was completed in October 1957. Gearbox failures prevented completion of a 10 hour test program until January 1958. In February taxi and tethered hovering flights were undertaken, however gearbox failures continued to plague the program. In June 1958 the VZ-3RY was shipped to the Ames Research Center, NASA, Moffett Field, California and from June to September 94 hours of full scale wind tunnel tests were taken. The VZ-3RY had a wingspan of 23 ft 5-in., length of 27 ft 8-in, height of 10 ft 8-in and gross weight of 2600 lb.

1 built, 1957

VZ-3RY — Configuration 2

As a result of the wind tunnel and thrust stand tests, the VZ-3RY was modified at Moffett by NASA personnel working under Ryan direction during October and December 1958. Modifications included installation of a nose landing gear and modification of the fuselage to carry the nose gear load; installation of flight test instruments; replacement of the gearboxes; installation of a ventral fin and replacement of upper and lower flaps. Thirteen flights were completed from the first flight date of Dec 29, 1958 through Feb 13, 1959. On that date the left propeller did not come out of flat pitch during a landing and the combination of loss of engine power and the windmilling propeller caused the VZ-3RY to hit the ground hard, wiping out landing gear, props and pylons.

(1 modified), 1958

VZ-3RY — Configuration 3 "Vertiplane"

In April 1959, Ryan was authorized to rebuild and modify the VZ-3RY. Returned to San Diego, the VZ-3RY had the following modifications made: fuselage extended forward of the wing; ejection seat (open cockpit) installed; main landing gear extended and tread widened; center support for lower flap installed; relocate thrust line parallel to wing chord; increase fuel capacity and install fuel boost pump and increase horizontal stabilizer span by 10 percent. First flight of the third configuration VZ-3RY was Dec 4, 1959. During subsequent flights the VZ-3RY achieved a zero airspeed in a hovering condition from 4000 feet to the ground. NASA undertook further flight tests after taking delivery of the aircraft on Jan 26, 1960. Shown in cockpit is NASA test pilot Ron Gerdes in photo taken May 23, 1962. In 1975 the VZ-3RY is on display at the Army Aviation Museum, Ft. Rucker, Alabama.

(1 modified), 1959

X-13 "Vertijet"   Experimental VTOL   2 built, 1955

There were two X-13 built as a follow-on to successful experiments with a tethered and winged J-33 jet engine begun by Ryan in 1947. Fitted with a temporary fixed landing gear, X-13 (s/n 54-1619) flew for the first time Dec 10, 1955. The second X-13 (s/n 54-1620) flew for the first time Nov 28, 1956. First complete VTOL flight sequence (vertical take-off from its "support" trailer, transition to horizontal flight, vertical landing) in the world was accomplished on April 11, 1957 by X-13 54-1620. The relatively small X-13 had a span of 21 ft, length of 24 ft and height of 15 ft. Weight was about 7500 lb and providing sufficient thrust for the vertical maneuvers was a single Rolls-Royce Avon of 10,000 lb s.t. Built for the Air Force, both X-13 survive; 54-1619 at the National Air and Space Museum and 54-1620 at the Air Force Museum, Dayton, Ohio.

Flexwing   Experimental   1 built, 1960

Designed as a manned flying research vehicle, the Ryan Flexwing (N140N) was designed to prove the flexible wing theory of Francis M. Rogallo. The Flexwing vehicle was part of a series of flexible wing flight articles, both manned and unmanned. First pilot of the Flexwing was Lou Everett. The wing was made by a sailmaker and was of Mylar bonded to nylon and mounted between an aluminum longitudinal keel and two tubular leading edges flexibly joined at the front end of the keel. It had a wingspan of 40 ft and derived its lift from the flow of air which inflated the sail. Engine was a 180 hp Lycoming. Test program lead to additional vehicles including the Fleep for the Army.

XV-8A Fleep   Experimental   1 built, 1963

As a follow-on article to the Flexwing program, Ryan built the XV-8A Fleep (63-19003 - Flexible Wing Aerial Utility Vehicle) for the U. S. Army. The Fleep needed only 500 ft ground roll for take off and not more than 100 ft with a 6 to 8 knot wind for landing. Engine was a 200 hp Continental with a fixed pitch prop. Like the Flexwing the Fleep was a two control vehicle with lateral and logitudinal but no rudder control.

XV-5A "Vertifan"   Experimental VTOL   2 built, 1952

Ryan was continually in the forefront of vertical and short field take-off/landing technology ever since the Dragonfly flew in 1939. The XV-5A for the Army (s/n 62-4506/4507) made over 388 flights and flew over 150 hours during the performance of eight flight test programs. First flying in 1964, the XV-5A had a rated speed of 456 knots forward, 22 knots to the rear and 30 sideways. First XV-5A crashed April 27, 1965 killing test pilot Lou Everett. Second XV-5A crashed on October 5, 1966 killing Air Force test pilot Major David H. Tittle, however aircraft was not badly damaged and was rebuilt as XV-5B.

XV-5B "Vertifan"　　　　　　　　Experimental VTOL　　　　　　　　(1 modified, 1967)

Following crash of the second XV-5A, it was rebuilt to the configuration of XV-5B (NASA 705). The landing gear was moved outboard of the wing fans, an improved seat was installed and VHF radio added. Ryan pilot Bill Anderson made first XV-5B flights. In 1976 XV-5B remains on standby readiness at NASA Ames Laboratory and available for flight. XV-5B was loaned to NASA by the Army to further pursue the fan-in-wing principle with an eye to future commercial requirements of reliability, safety and performance. XV-5B had a 12,500 lb conventional and 11,000 lb vertical gross take-off weight. In addition to Vertifan program, Ryan was deeply involved in the XC-142 tilt-wing transport project, building wings, fuselage and tail assembly in partnership with Ling-Temco-Vought and Hiller.

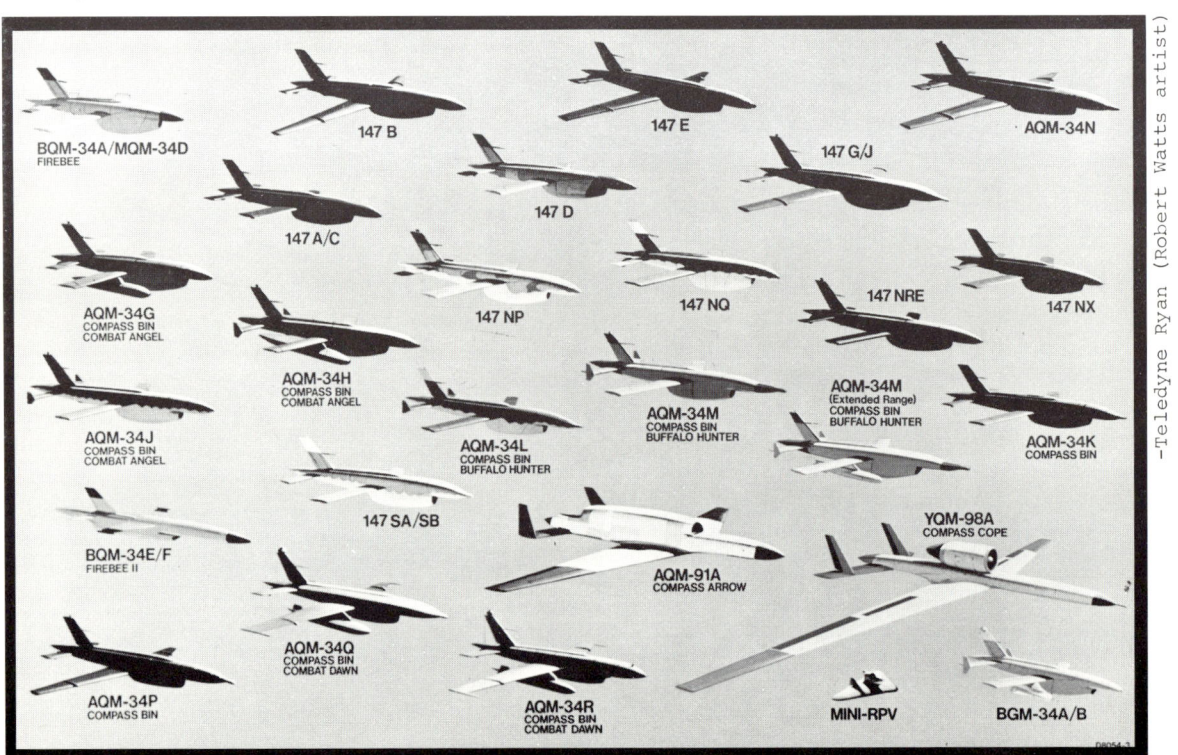

RPV (Various)　　　　　　　　Uses vary

From the Firebee of 1947 (first contract) to the Compass Cope of 1975, Ryan has been the leader in the development of RPV's — Remotely Piloted Vehicles, which may well be the wave of the future in high-risk military aircraft hardware. The names are exotic, Firebee, Red Wagon, Compass Dawn, and Firefly, and the performances are spectacular, "over 60,000 ft" altitude, "Mach 2" and "around the world". It is not beyond reality that tomorrow's "Aces" will be military pilots flying Ryan interceptors, sitting safely in bunkers a long way from combat and the guy that gets shot down has to pay off in beer not blood. The Ryan RPV family began with simple recoverable target drones for pilot intercept proficiency training. The drones or RPV's are numbered in a "family". The Firebee I target drone is Model 124, the Firebee II is 166, the reconnaissance drone family is Model 147, the Firefly is Model 154.

THE OLD WORDS . . . .

Nostalgia . . . . is defined as a longing for something far away or long ago. Aviation history has moved so fast that events just a few years old can be considered "long ago" and we are often moved by the thoughts of the "good old days." Taking a look at the old days; at the old words and old pictures put on us to make us buy or fly these airplanes is good, for it puts into perspective the events that have followed. Taking a fresh look at these old words and pictures we can once more relive the time — not so long ago at all — when flying was an adventure for the bold spirited man or woman. Maybe to those who read this — it still is. We hope so.

THEN and NOW

ON "The Spirit of St. Louis" was a Standard Steel Propeller when it made its great flights.

NOW—the choice of Colonel Lindbergh, based on experience and preference, is another Mahoney monoplane equipped with the same type of propeller.

Follow the choice of experience!

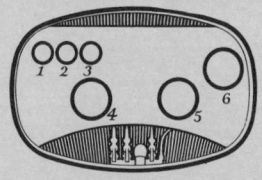

STANDARD STEEL PROPELLER CO.
PITTSBURGH, PENNSYLVANIA

MAHONEY PLANES are Money Makers
SISTERSHIPS TO THE SPIRIT OF ST. LOUIS

YOU are in line for greater profits with the Mahoney dealer franchise than with any other plane. Transportation and aerial taxi companies know that in the Sistership to the "Spirit of St. Louis"...

THE MOST ADVERTISED PLANE IN THE WORLD

...they have a *great drawing card*, a plane that has the admiration and confidence of everybody! Corporations are more and more active in the acquisition of this type of plane for their executives. Sportsmen and individuals of wealth find it ideal for week-end trips and long distance hops across the country. There's *a great market* for the Ryan Brougham!

Dealer franchises will be increasingly difficult to obtain. Send your application today for the territory you desire, and it will receive immediate attention.

MUTUAL AIRCRAFT CORPORATION
363 South Olive Street · · LOS ANGELES
Telephone MUtual 1131
Western Distributors for Mahoney Aircraft Corporation

RANKIN FLYING SERVICE
Representative for Oregon, Washington, and Idaho
Municipal Airport on Greeley St., Portland, Ore.

Six Consolidated Instruments
On Lindbergh's New Ryan Brougham

1. Air pressure gauge
2. Temperature gauge
3. Oil pressure gauge
4. Tachometer
5. Air speed indicator
6. Altimeter

THE reproduction above is from an actual photograph of the instrument board of Colonel Charles Lindbergh's new Ryan Brougham. With the accompanying explanatory diagram it shows the exact position of each of the *six* Consolidated Instruments with which Lindbergh's new ship — like *all* Ryan airplanes — is equipped.

Consolidated dash lights and navigation lights are also employed on this flashing successor to the world-famed "Spirit of St. Louis."

One or more Consolidated Instruments is standard equipment on most American commercial airplanes — an eloquent tribute to the dependability of our products.

CONSOLIDATED
INSTRUMENT COMPANY OF AMERICA, INC.
41 East 42nd Street, New York
Western Representative— M. E. HULSE, 5391 Broadway, Oakland, Calif.

Altimeters, Tachometers, Oil Pressure Gauges, Gasoline Gauges, Thermometers, Air Speed Indicators, Compasses, Navigation Lights, Landing Lights, Dash Lights, etc.

Col. Charles A. Lindbergh's new airplane is equipped with Goodyear Tires

GOODYEAR
The Greatest Name in Rubber

AIRCRAFT OF THE FIGHTING POWERS - 1940

AERO DIGEST, January 1940

AMERICA'S OUTSTANDING MODERN SPORT AND TRAINING PLANE — FEATURING ALL METAL FUSELAGE, WING FLAPS AND THE FAMOUS MENASCO ENGINE. OUTPERFORMS EVERY PLANE IN ITS HORSEPOWER CLASS RYAN AERONAUTICAL COMPANY, SAN DIEGO, CALIFORNIA

AERO DIGEST, April 1935

Ryan S-T

Wing flaps lower approximately 30°. The new flap control gives accurate, split-second adjustment and simplifies precision landings.

Both cockpits are roomy and comfortably upholstered. Back of seat in front cockpit hinges forward as shown to give access to 40 lb. baggage compartment.

TO YOU... sportsman pilot, commercial opera[tor] and flying school owner—the Ryan Aeronautical Compa[ny] offers the improved 1937 Ryan S-T series, including the S[-T,] S-T-A and S-T-A Special Models, with high performance a[nd] low operating costs that set a new standard of all arou[nd] excellence.

The new Ryan S-T airplanes are outstanding in their field, [as] were their famous predecessors which carried, as did C[ol.] Lindbergh's "Spirit of St. Louis," the name of Ryan to all p[arts] of the world. Built by T. Claude Ryan, the founder of Ry[an] Aeronautical activities, the Ryan S-T incorporates the [most] experience gained through nineteen years of intensive ae[ro]nautical progress.

ADVANCED DESIGN. Fully a third faster in cruising sp[eed] for comparable power, the Ryan S-T also combines slow la[nd]ing speeds and unusual economy of operation. To gain [this] remarkable efficiency, Ryan engineers have utilized the la[test] proven developments in aircraft design and constructi[on] previously available only in the most modern high sp[eed] transport planes.

A QUALITY SPORT AIRPLANE. The new Ryan, designe[d to] meet the requirements of true sport flying, is a modern [air]plane of the most practical size for the private owner. The [real] pleasure of flying varies widely with different airplanes. [To] fly the Ryan S-T is, for the veteran as well as the amateur, [to] discover a new joy and thrill. Cross-country flying at h[igh] speed with stability, maneuverability, and slow landing sp[eed] for small airports, gives a delight and satisfaction [un]approached in ordinary aircraft. The Ryan S-T has b[een] called the plane with perfect handling qualities.

A PROFIT-MAKING TRAINING PLANE. The same combi[na]tion of qualities that make the new Ryan S-T ideal for sp[orts]man pilots, also makes this airplane superior for trai[ning] purposes. Flying characteristics in all maneuvers are excel[lent] and students quickly gain an easy "feel" of the plane.

1937 Ryan Brochure

attracts student and rental business in volume, experience has shown it to be an outstanding money-maker on any airport. The new Ryan is one of the easiest planes to fly. Extraordinary stability—laterally, longitudinally, and directionally—is inherent in these ships and they can be flown indefinitely with hands or feet off the controls. Likewise the S-T is entirely free from any ground looping tendencies. Its effective wing flaps (air brakes) reduce the actual landing speed and make it much easier to get into small fields.

ECONOMY. The pleasure or the profit of owning an airplane is greatly enhanced by a truly low operating cost. The new Ryan, with its high aerodynamic efficiency, gives seventeen miles per gallon of gas at 125 miles per hour, while the metal fuselage, with its extra strong construction throughout, keeps maintenance down to the very minimum.

MANEUVERABILITY. Practically every known aerobatic maneuver can be performed easily with the Ryan S-T. It must be forced into a spin maneuver and recovers instantly at the will of the pilot. This ship has an exceptionally high structural safety factor throughout, giving an extra sense of security to the owner even though he may never wish to do more than a steep bank.

VISION. The oval cross-sectioned fuselage and the low, narrow chord wing give the pilot and passenger maximum possible vision.

COMFORT. Cockpits are exceptionally roomy. Full bulkheads between seats eliminate drafts. Cockpits are designed for use with seat type parachutes or with kapok filled cushions, the latter of which are standard. Upholstering is in red leatherette.

CONSTRUCTION

FUSELAGE. The fuselage is of all-metal, monocoque type construction, using thick gauge Alclad 17ST and 24ST skin. This strong Alclad metal is highly resistant to damage and deterioration, and eliminates forever the annoyance of recovering with fabric and dope.

WINGS. The thoroughly modern Ryan wing construction is impressive in the soundness of its engineering and unusual strength. Aluminum alloy ribs, steel compression members, and spruce spars comprise the framework. Covering is of fabric with the leading edge of the wing sheathed in 17ST metal as far back as the front spar. Thus, preservation of the true airfoil is assured. Due to the design, either front or rear spar may be replaced without damage to any rib or fitting—a point of considerable advantage in repair operations.

AILERONS. Aileron construction incorporates a steel tube spar, aluminum alloy ribs, and fabric cover. The leading edge is covered with 17ST Alclad.

Dual controls are provided. Those in the front cockpit are removable. Note the wing flap control lever at the right. The instruments shown are standard, except Turn and Bank indicator.

1937 Ryan Brochure

AUXILIARY GAS TANK. An auxiliary removable gas tank, offered as optional equipment, is built to fit snugly on the seat in the front cockpit. This 16 gallon capacity tank increases the cruising range to 600 miles. For use with this extra tank, a metal cockpit cover is available. This hinges open for baggage and is removable at will. The use of the cover gives smooth lines and eliminates front cockpit drag.

BAGGAGE COMPARTMENT. The back of the seat in the front cockpit hinges forward to give access to the baggage compartment. The compartment follows the contour of the fuselage and is approximately 26" wide by 20" high by 11⅜" deep. There is ample room for two overnight bags and other miscellaneous equipment. A Sesame combination lock is standard.

WING FLAPS. Wing flaps are and always have been standard equipment on the Ryan S-T. Flaps may be lowered to an angle of 30° A new flap control is a feature of the 1937 models. A lever on the right-hand side of the cockpit, which operates as simply and directly as an automobile brake, provides split-second adjustment to any one of five positions. Precision landings are greatly simplified.

TAIL SURFACES. Tail surfaces are of riveted 17ST aluminum alloy with covering of fabric. The use of modern trimming tabs on both elevators permits a more precise longitudinal balance. Their adjustment from either cockpit is positive and effective. Any desired setting may be obtained. The tabs make possible a strong rigid stabilizer, which eliminates all possibility of high speed flutter.

CONTROLS. Complete dual controls, with dual brakes, are standard equipment. Those in the front cockpit are quickly removable. The design of the entire control system has been refined to a high degree of simplicity and direct action with large bearing areas and ball bearings at vital points. A highly polished chrome stick and wing flap control lever are attractive additions to the appearance of the well arranged cockpit.

LANDING GEAR. The landing gear is of treadle type with 18" x 8" x 3" full air wheels, mechanical brakes and long stroke oleo shock absorbers. Wheel pants are of 17ST and far more durable than the conventional aluminum type. The landing gear tread is 66", which, with the low center of gravity of the entire plane, makes the S-T very stable on the ground. The tail wheel is pneumatic and full swiveling. The new tail wheel swivel lock, controlled from the pilot's cockpit, makes ground looping virtually impossible.

ENGINE. Menasco Pirate engines of 95 h.p., 125 h.p., and 150 h.p., are standard equipment of the Ryan S-Ts. The 150 h.p. engine is supercharged.

These four cylinder, in-line, aircooled power plants are known throughout the world for their brilliant racing performance and ruggedness. The Menasco gives exceptionally long service between overhauls and is highly reliable and long-lived The smooth operation of the engine together with the special rubber mounting effectively dampens vibration. Complete elimination of exhaust gases and lessening of motor noise is achieved by the low position of the exhaust outlet.

1937 Ryan Brochure

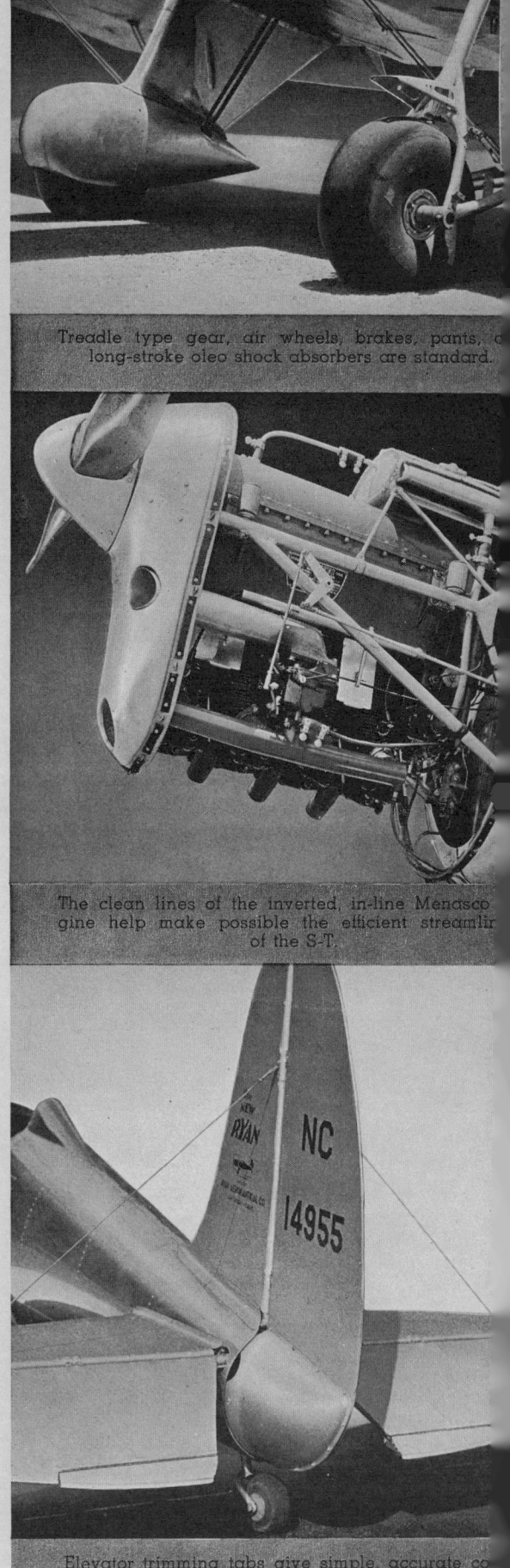

Treadle type gear, air wheels, brakes, pants, and long-stroke oleo shock absorbers are standard.

The clean lines of the inverted, in-line Menasco engine help make possible the efficient streamlining of the S-T.

Elevator trimming tabs give simple, accurate co[ntrol]. The full swiveling, pneumatic tail wheel is equi[pped] with shock absorber and tail wheel lock.

STANDARD EQUIPMENT

All models of the 1937 Series are exceptionally well equipped and include many features as standard and which would otherwise cost $600 to $700 as "extras."

- Wing flaps with new, instant lever control.
- Tab balance controls.
- Wheel pants, wing fillets and fairing throughout.
- N.A.C.A. in-line engine cowling.
- Full swiveling, pneumatic tail wheel.
- Tail wheel swivel lock, controlable from cockpit.
- Full airwheels.
- Wheel brakes, controlled from both cockpits.
- Long stroke, oleo type shock absorbers.
- Wiring for position lights.
- Baggage compartment.
- Sesame combination lock.
- Direct reading fuel gauge.
- Reserve fuel supply system.
- Complete set dual controls.
- Impulse hand starter.
- Altimeter.
- Tachometer.
- Compass.
- Airspeed indicator.
- Oil pressure gauge.
- Oil temperature gauge.
- First aid kit.
- Fire extinguisher.
- Tool kit.
- Aircraft and Engine Log Book.
- Aircraft and Engine Instruction Manuals.
- Parachute type seats.
- Attractive cockpit upholstering, including thick cushions and back pads.

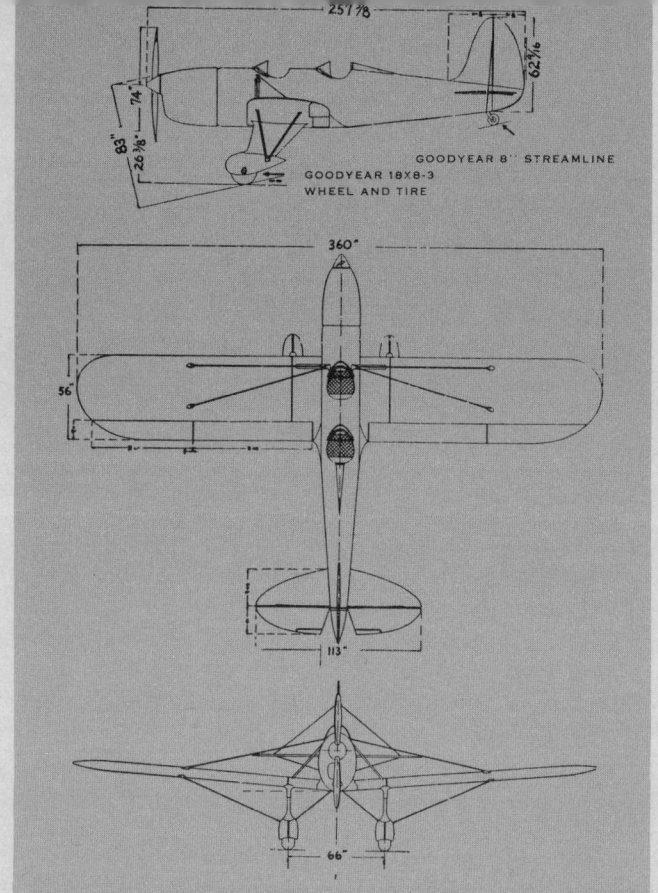

FOREIGN SHIPMENT

All models of the new Ryan S-T series when boxed for foreign shipment are carefully treated with a special cosmoline coating and wrapped as an extra preventative against salt water exposure. Wings and tail surfaces are disassembled and the plane and motor placed in one box of the following dimensions:

	English	Metric
Length	20' 4"	6.20 M
Width	6' 3"	1.91 M
Height	4' 8"	1.42 M
Total Weight	2400 lbs.	1088 kg.
Total Content	593 cu. ft.	16.8 M³

SPECIFICATIONS AND PERFORMANCE

Models S-T, S-T-A, and S-T-A Special

Model	S-T	S-T-A	S-T-A Special
Engine—Menasco	B-4	C-4	C-4-S (Supercharged)
Horsepower	95 H.P. at 1975 R.P.M.	125 H.P. at 2175 R.P.M.	150 H.P. at 2275 R.P.M.
Wing Span	30'	30'	30'
Length Overall	21' 5 3/8"	21' 5 3/8"	21' 5 3/8"
Height Overall	6' 11"	6' 11"	6' 11"
Wing Area	124 sq. ft.	124 sq. ft.	124 sq. ft.
Fuel Capacity	24 gal.	24 gal.	24 gal.
Fuel Consumption per hr.	7 gal.	8 gal.	8.6 gal.
Propeller Clearance—Level	23.75"	23.75"	22.25"
Airfoil Section	N.A.C.A. 2412	N.A.C.A. 2412	N.A.C.A. 2412
Wheel Tread	66"	66"	66"
Tire Size (Air wheels)	18 x 8-3	18 x 8-3	18 x 8-3
Tail Wheel Size	8" Pneumatic	8" Pneumatic	8" Pneumatic
Weight Empty	1023 lbs.	1023 lbs.	1058 lbs.
Useful Load	552 lbs.	552 lbs.	517 lbs.
Gross Load (Maximum)	1575 lbs.	1575 lbs.	1575 lbs.
Range (Cruising)	400 mi.	350 mi.	350 mi.
Maximum Speed at Sea Level	140 M.P.H.	150 M.P.H.	160 M.P.H.
Cruising Speed at 2000 ft.	120 M.P.H.	127 M.P.H.	135 M.P.H.
Rate of Climb (Sea Level)	850 ft./min.	1200 ft./min.	1400 ft./min.
Service Ceiling	15,500 ft.	17,500 ft.	21,000 ft.
Landing Speed	42 M.P.H.	42 M.P.H.	42 M.P.H.
Landing Speed with Flaps Up	50 M.P.H.	50 M.P.H.	50 M.P.H.
Take-off Run with Full Load	190 yds.	175 yds.	145 yds.

RYAN AERONAUTICAL COMPANY
LINDBERGH FIELD, SAN DIEGO, CALIFORNIA
CABLE ADDRESS "RYANCO"

1937 Ryan Brochure

POPULAR AVIATION, November 1934

YOUNG MRS. ROCKEFELLER PILOTS A LOW-WING MONOPLANE

Mrs. John W. Rockefeller, Jr., of New York and Allenhurst, is an aviation enthusiast. She favors jodhpurs, windbreaker, and close-fitting helmet. Flies a low-wing monoplane. Has had several thrilling experiences in the air, one of which she tells about. "I've been caught in heavy fog," she says, "with vision less than ten yards. That's enough to shatter anybody's nerves. My first thought, when I put my feet on firm ground, was to smoke a Camel. Smoking Camels eases up my nervous tension—sets me right again. I can smoke all I like—and they never tire my taste. 'I'd walk a mile for a Camel'—and *fly* a thousand!"

Cigarette advertising late 1930's

Flying Equipment

What's new in aircraft, engines and major accessories

Ryan's New ST Series

Three ships are offered with Menasco power plants of 95, 125 and 150 hp.

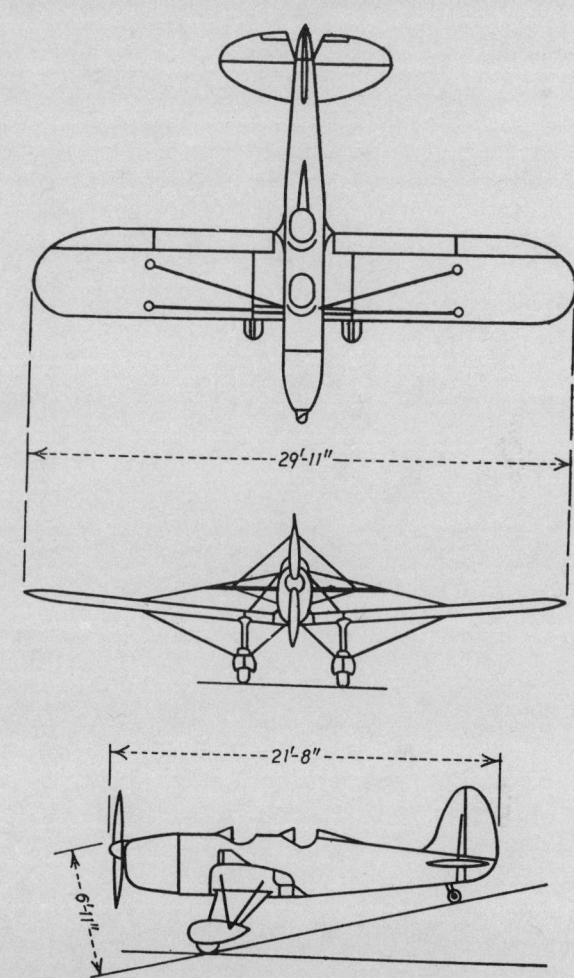

AFTER THE CLOSE of the midsummer ATA maintenance meeting (news Section) we dropped down to San Diego and spent the best part of a day with Claude Ryan and Earl Prudden at their Lindbergh Field base. The Ryan Aeronautical Company shops were busy turning out 1936 versions of the Model ST two-seater. Already they have produced as many ships this year as they did in the entire year of 1935.

High spot of the visit was a chance to fly the new ST. We went out with John Fornasero, Ryan's chief test pilot. We followed him through for a take-off and a landing, and then tried a couple ourselves which turned out not too badly, considering that we have done comparatively little active flying of late. The ship is a joy to fly. She is light and quick on the controls, but stable enough so that it does not have to be flown constantly even in fairly gusty weather. She made good turns, "feet off," and would fly comfortably "hands off" for extended periods. Fore and aft trim by means of the elevator tabs was found to be very effective.

Lateral control at stall was unusually good. Stalled, power off or power on, the ship responded quickly to lateral stick movements, and showed no tendency to slip off into a spin, right or left. Spin qualities appear to be good regardless of position of the flap. Recovery is quick. As flap is lowered time for recovery decreases.

In landing, with the flap full down, we found no evidence of tail buffeting or blanketing, the ship being under positive longitudinal control at all times. The flap makes possible a steep approach glide. The actual landing speed appeared to be reasonably low, and the ground run, with full brake application was very short.

Ryan ST Models for 1936, similar in general appearance to their predecessors, incorporate a number of improvements.

AVIATION, August 1936

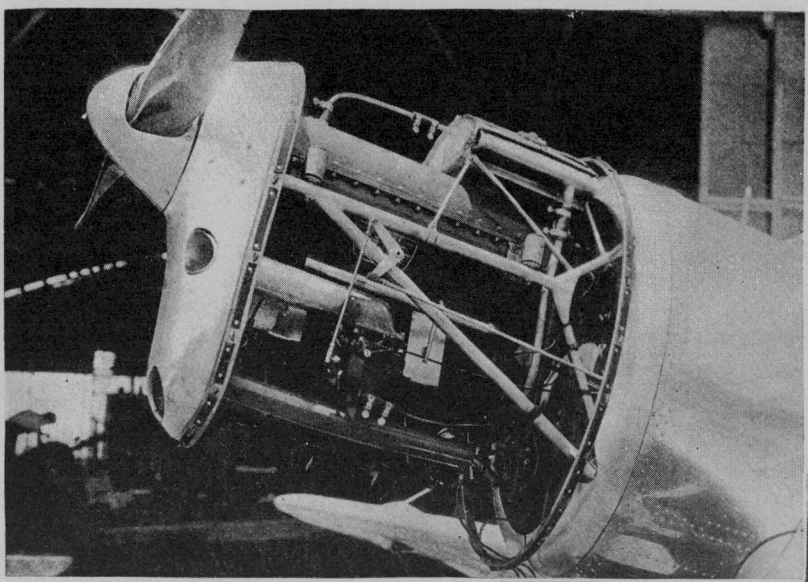

With cowling removed, the Menasco power plants are easily accessible for servicing. The entire installation detaches from the stainless steel firewall by removing four bolts. The engine fastens to the bearers through rubber bushings.

minum assemblies in the ship. It is of a built-up welded sheet steel and carries the front spar fittings as well as the points of attachment for the diagonal wing bracing struts and the upper bracing wires.

The whole engine installation forward of the stainless steel fire wall comes off as a unit by disconnecting four main bolts and the engine controls. This power unit is of simple design, clean cut, and makes the whole engine completely accessible for servicing when the cowlings are removed. A simple modification of the engine bearers takes

Thanks to the oval fuselage section, vision from either cockpit is excellent. The wing is set well aft and does not interfere seriously with the field of vision forward and downward. We flew from the rear, but had no trouble at all in seeing all that was necessary of the ground as we approached by very little movement of the head. Cockpits are narrow, but are plenty wide enough for comfort. The windshield designs are such that cockpits are free of any objectionable airblast.

Controls are simple and do not clutter up the cockpit. Heel actuated brake pedals are attached to the rudder pedals. Elevator tab control is obtained by moving fore and aft a light cable that runs through the cockpit just under the throttle. A short lever for locking the swiveling tail wheel (during cross-wind landings) is located on the floor just beside the stick. Older ST models had the flap control in the form of a short crank located near the floor on the right-hand side of the rear cockpit, but new models carry a direct-acting lever in about the same location.

Details of the under-carriage. Goodyear Airwheels are carried on long travel oleos. Of interest is the cluster fitting for the tie-rods. Pants and other fairings are now made of drophammer formed Alclad dural.

Pulling the lever full back puts the flap full down—throwing the lever forward puts the flap back into normal position. Flaps can be locked in any intermediate position also. The action is much faster than with the older crank-type installation. The seats are of the bucket type arranged to take seat-pack parachutes. They are fitted with comfortable backs and head rests. Instrument board arrangement is simple and efficient.

Going down the Ryan factory production line, we were struck by the rugged simplicity of the ship in all its parts. The fuselage is of a full monocoque pattern. Skin plating is of heavy gage Alclad riveted to drophammer-formed dural rings. There are no fore and aft members except for a couple of inverted U sections riveted inside the skin running from the upper engine mount connections at the fire wall to points aft of the rear cockpit to carry the loads around the cockpit openings. Most ingenious is the main fuselage ring located just ahead of the front cockpit, one of the few non-alu-

care of the three alternate Menasco power plants. As a result of continuous research, the 1936 STs have a new type of engine baffling which provides adequate cooling under all possible conditions of outside temperature.

Landing gear of the latest STs is basically the same as for older models. Main wheels are 18x8x3 Goodyear Airwheels with mechanically operated brakes. Shock absorbers are of the oleo type. All bearings are fitted with bronze bushings readily replaceable. Tail wheel is 8 in. in diameter, streamlined, mounted on a trombone type rubber shock absorber. It is full swiveling, with lock controllable from the cockpit. A recent improvement is the manufacture of all pants and fairings of Alclad dural instead of the softer aluminum sheet formerly used. The drop-hammer-formed Alclad is stiff and rigid, and withstands normal wear and tear readily. Pants are quickly removable for wheel and brake inspection.

Wings are of the same general type of construction as former models with solid spruce spars, aluminum alloy

Tail surfaces are aluminum alloy framed, fabric covered. Elevator tabs give effective longitudinal trim.

POWER PLANT — MENASCO	S-T B4 — 95 h.p. @ 1,975 r.p.m.	S-T-A C4 — 125 h.p. @ 2,175 r.p.m.	S-T-A- SPECIAL C4S — 150 h.p. @ 2,275 r.p.m.
Wing Span	29 ft. 11 in.	29 ft. 11 in.	29 ft. 11 in.
Length Overall	21 ft. 8 in.	21 ft. 8 in.	21 ft. 8 in.
Height Overall	6 ft. 11 in.	6 ft. 11 in.	6 ft. 11 in.
Wing Area	124 sq. ft.	124 sq. ft.	124 sq. ft.
Propeller Diameter	77 in.	77 in.	80 in.
Airfoil Section	N.A.C.A. 2412	N.A.C.A. 2412	N.A.C.A. 2412
Weight Empty	1,027 lb.	1,027 lb.	
Useful Load	539 lb.	539 lb.	
Gross Load (Maximum)	1,575 lb.	1,575 lb.	1,575 lb.
Range	400 mi.	375 mi.	375 mi.
Maximum Speed @ Sea Level	140 m.p.h.	150 m.p.h.	160 m.p.h. (not yet accurately tested)
Maximum Speed @ 7,500 ft.	128 m.p.h.	137 m.p.h.	148 m.p.h.
Cruising Speed @ 2,000 ft.	120 m.p.h.	127 m.p.h.	138 m.p.h.
Rate of Climb (Sea Level)	850 ft./min.	1,200 ft./min.	1,400 ft./min.
Service Ceiling	15,500 ft.	17,000 ft.	21,000 ft.
Landing Speed	42 m.p.h.	42 m.p.h.	42 m.p.h.
Take-off Run — full load	190 yd.	175 yd.	145 yd.

Ryan

RYAN B-5: 6-place; J6-9. 50 hours since major. Bendix wheels and brakes, new tires, tubes. Ship excellent condition. Complete instruments. Engine ring. Will trade. $1,650. C. Strong, 3024 South Parkway, Chicago, Illinois.

FOR SALE: Ryan B-1, 5-place; J-5 powered. Licensed to June 1938. Landing lights, electric starter, 12-volt battery, rate of climb, bank and turn, large tail group. Rubbed finish. $900. Elwyn West, Route 3, Appleton, Wisconsin.

RYAN: 5-place cabin; J-5, just topped; ship completely rebuilt last spring; full streamlined; speed ring; cruises 110. Best J-5 Ryan in country. $1,400. Will trade. Northern Oklahoma Flying Service, Blackwell, Oklahoma.

FOR SALE: Ryan B-1, J-5 engine. Metal prop; equipped with RCA radio; 3-minute electric flares, landing and navigation lights, large battery and box. Ship licensed to August 2, 1938. Will sell less equipment and less motor. Thomas Brothers Air Service, Detroit City Airport, Detroit, Mich.

RYAN B-1, J-5: Five-place. Silver with red trimmings. Very good condition. $975. $487 down. Will take trade. St. Louis Flying Service, Inc., Lambert Field, St. Louis, Missouri.

RYAN B-5: J6-9; 120 hours since major of engine. Completely equipped for aerial mapping. Would also be efficient for dusting. Located Omaha, Nebraska. Price, $1,500. Ryan B-3: J6-9. 100 hours since major of engine. Can be licensed for six-place with J-5. Completely equipped for aerial mapping. Ideal for barnstorming small fields. Price, $1,400. Located Teterboro Airport. Both planes owned by Standard Aerial Surveys, Inc., Hackensack, N. J.

B-1 RYAN J-5: Cabin monoplane, 5-place, excellent condition; full of extras. Licensed to September 1937. $975. May consider trade or finance. Fred Rigler, 1049 Lincoln Place, Brooklyn, N. Y.

ST-A RYAN: 1937, NC17300. 125 hp Menasco motor. All standard factory instruments, including compass. Electric starter, booster, battery; wired for lights. $4,500. AERO DIGEST, Box 2616.

RYAN B-7: Wasp C, 420 hp. Six-place. Manufactured in 1930. Licensed to October 1937. Excellent condition. Has red velvet upholstering, landing lights, rate of climb, tail wheel, battery box, hand inertia starter and air speed. 760 hours total time on ship. 45 hours since overhaul on engine by Braniff Airways. $1,475; $700 down; $79 a month for 12 months. Will take trade. St. Louis Flying Service, Inc., Lambert Field, St. Louis, Mo.

RYAN B-1, J-5: Licensed to September 15, 1937. Large gas tanks. Silver trimmed in red. Airwheels, bank and turn, tail wheel. Geared starter. 110 hours since major on ship, 50 hours since major on engine. Excellent condition. $50 a month for 12 months. Will take trade. St. Louis Flying Service, Inc., Lambert Field, St. Louis, Missouri.

REPOSSESSED B-1 RYAN cabin ship, less motor. Price, $450. Repossessed J-5 6-place Stinson cabin ship; price, $550. Repossessed 330 hp Stinson, with or without motor. Make offer with or without motor. Bargain prices. Edw. A. Forner, Jackson, Michigan.

RYAN B-7: Licensed to October '37. Condition perfect. Wasp B motor, 21 hours since factory majored. Electric and hand inertia starter. Folding wing, landing lights; upholstery perfect. As new ship. Cannot be appreciated without seeing. Price, $2,500. or will trade for two 40-B Boeings, J-5 Travel Airs or Stearmans. Finklea Brothers, Leland, Mississippi.

RYAN STA: 125 hp. Menasco; perfect condition throughout; less than 200 hours; no cracks; always hangared. Priced at $3,000 at Minneapolis. W. M. Miller, Cloquet, Minn.

AERO DIGEST - 1937 issues

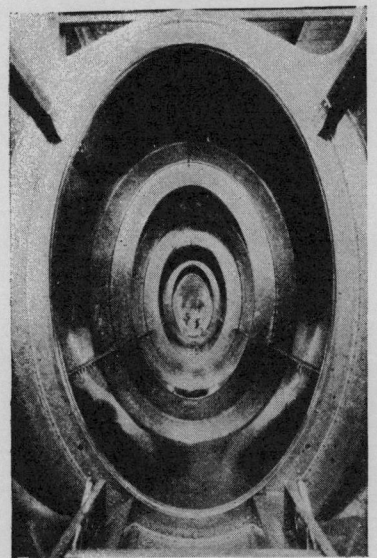

Fuselage construction is simplicity itself. This view shows the section from the rear cockpit to the tail cone. In the upper corners can be seen the U channels which carry the loads around cockpit openings.

ribs, steel compression members and fabric covering. Leading edge is covered with 17ST sheet to a point well back of the front spar. Ailerons have steel tube spars with aluminum alloy ribs, with leading edges covered with dural. They are push-pull tube operated, with differential action. Flaps are of similar construction to the ailerons. By the lever action described, they lower to a maximum of 30 deg. Tail surfaces are constructed entirely of aluminum alloys in the form of tubular spars and stamped ribs. Elevators and rudder are of the same construction. The entire assembly is fabric covered.

In addition to the wheel pants mentioned above, all motor cowling, fillets and other fairings formerly made of ordinary aluminum sheet are now made up from 17S or 24S Alclad, which are considerably stronger and more durable. Alclad shapes do not have the tendency to harden and crack which is exhibited by some of the materials formerly employed. The installation of drop-hammers and of improved sheet metal forming processes have made these changes possible.

An optional feature now being widely used is an auxiliary gas tank which can be placed in the front cockpit instead of a passenger to increase the range of the ship from 400 to 650 miles. This tank can be installed or removed quickly. It is Department of Commerce approved and does not affect the total weight or balance of the airplane. For use with the front seat tank installation, a removable front cockpit cover is available which hinges open for baggage.

Three models are now available all manufactured under Department of Commerce ATC Nos. 541 and 571. The general specifications and performance figures are given above.

AVIATION, January 1936

AERO DIGEST, April 1935

AVIATION, January 1936

AVIATION, March 1936

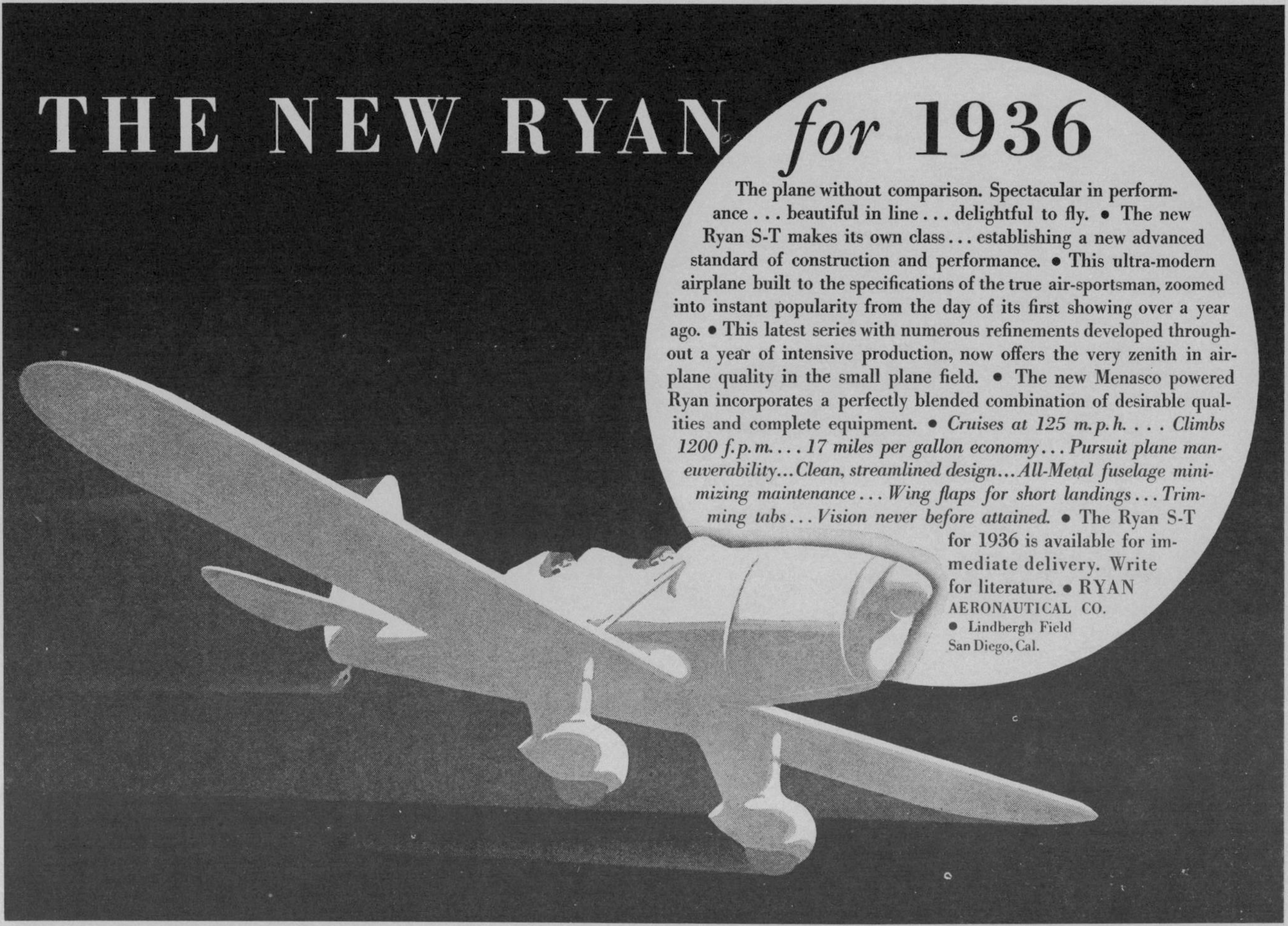

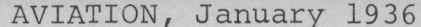

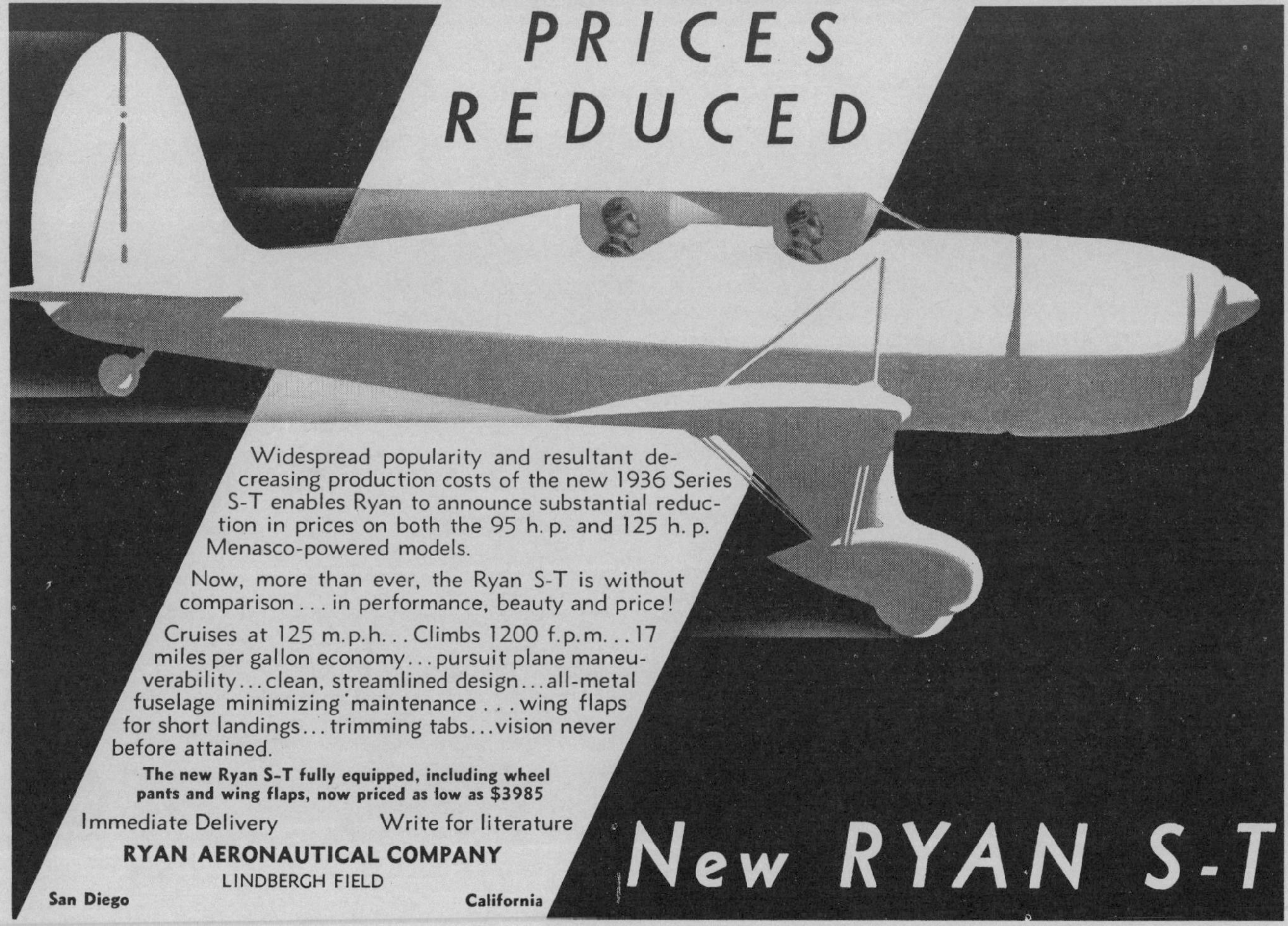

RYAN ST-M

The World's Leading Training Plane, used by the air forces of progressive nations throughout the world. Proven superior for both primary and advanced training. Modern metal construction, perfect flight characteristics, moderate in price, and lowest in operating and maintenance costs.

Cable Address
RYANCO

RYAN AERONAUTICAL CO., LINDBERGH FIELD, SAN DIEGO, CALIF.

AVIATION, November 1938

Ryan

The efficiency of the high performing, economically operated metal Ryan S-T type for modern pilot training has been recognized in the purchase by the U. S. Army Air Corps as well as by the air forces of many other progressive countries. Ryan Aeronautical Company, Lindbergh Field, San Diego, California, U.S.A.

CONTRACTORS TO THE U. S. ARMY AIR CORPS

AVIATION, July 1939

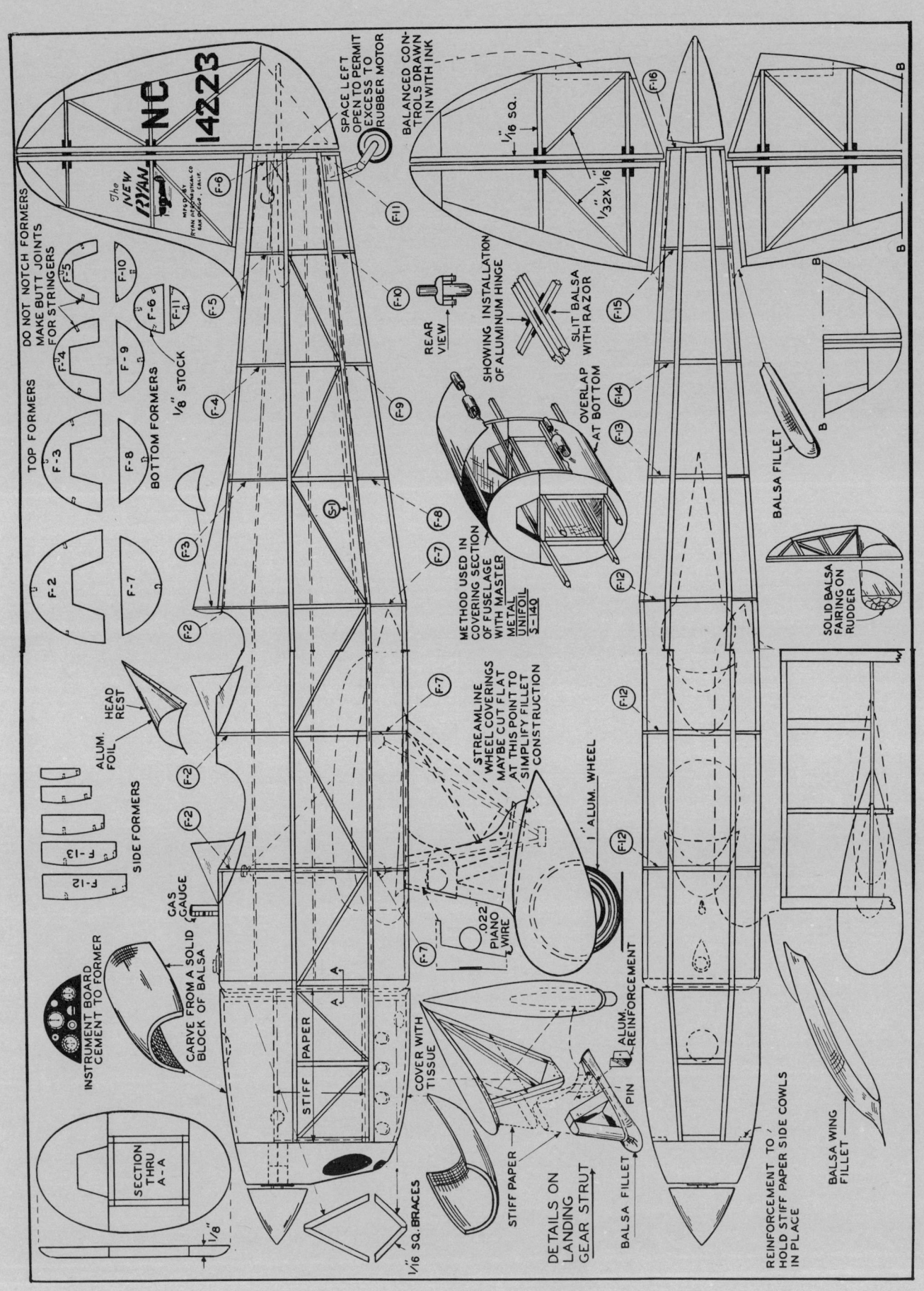

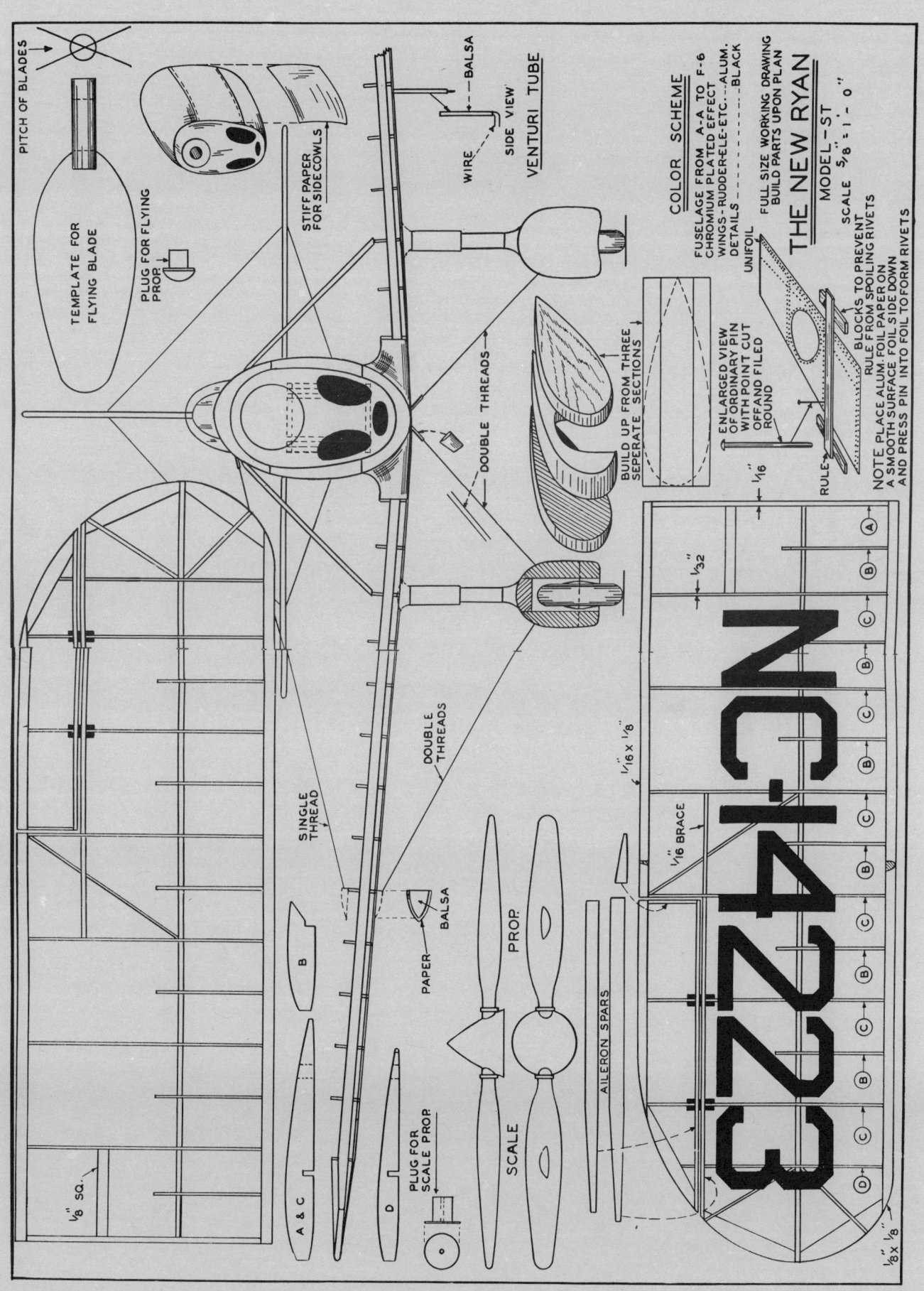

MENASCO OVER POPOCATEPTL

Wherever the going is tough, Menasco engines daily prove their championship performance, stamina and dependability. True to this tradition, the Menasco 150 h.p. supercharged engines that power the Mexican Air Force fleet of Ryan trainers are doing an outstanding job. Taking off from Mexico City at 7,200 feet and flying in formation over Popocateptl (Mexico's highest extinct volcano) these engines must deliver faultless performance at well over 18,000 feet. Whether your choice is the husky 50 h.p. Menasco for light planes or the sleek in-line 260 h.p. supercharged Menasco, you can be certain that no engines in the world are more expertly engineered, manufactured with finer precision or tested with greater care. Menasco Manufacturing Co., Los Angeles, California.

ANY AIRPLANE SELLS BETTER WHEN POWERED BY MENASCO

NOTE: Anyone having a copy of the original handbook of maneuvers described here is requested to please contact the publisher.

Air Corps Primary Training at a Civilian School

FLYING CADET WARREN S. BEALL

For many years the Air Corps primary flight school at Randolph Field has been acknowledged to have the world's finest course. Now, with the expanded Army pilot training program, primary training has been transferred from the "West Point of the Air" to nine selected civilian schools. To answer some of the questions which may arise concerning the success of the new program and the maintenance of the same high training standards, the writer is setting down some of the highlights of his recently completed primary training course. Perhaps these impressions will give older and wiser pilots—and fledgling fliers yet to come—an insight into the lessons we are learning

● Most flying cadets enter their careers in somewhat the same way I did, and with somewhat the same preconceived ideas. Newly-enrolled cadets in the primary stage (Dodos) are an eager group filled with the desire to become military pilots, but if their combined flying knowledge was placed end to end it would undoubtedly add up to little more than zero.

Hence, with a log of 65 hours on the Army's Ryan YPT-16 low-wing trainers and with successful completion of the Air Corps' primary course at the Ryan School of Aeronautics, I look down the ladder, and present this brief sketch of whys and wherefors.

Here's the way our first ten hours in *Primary Stage* line up:

Use of controls; Straight and level flight; Confidence maneuvers; Coordination exercises; Climbs and climbing turns; Glides and gliding turns; Gentle and medium turns; Stalls, power on and power off; Spins; Figure S patterns; Rectangular patterns; Take-offs and landings; Forced landings; Solo.

This glossary—today—looks somewhat obvious until I pause and reflect. And then out of cold, hard terminology come the fibers that weave the warp and woof of that high perfection in flying technique that must be required of service pilots. Hence, to me:

Use of Controls means more than a knowledge of which control surface moves as I move a cockpit control lever. I see a perfectly balanced plane, flying itself along a true level flight path until I, as its guide, bring about a change in pattern. I move the stick lightly to the left, and the left wing drops with my pressure. I press the left rudder pedal at the same time and I have built a well banked turn. My plane holds to its new curved course until I straighten it out with a movement of right stick and rudder. I climb with backward pressure on the stick and I descend with the amount of forward pressure I exert.

Simple as that? Not quite, for it has taken me most of my 65 hours to acquire the innate sense of timing and the delicate sense of pressures necessary for smooth, unbroken flight paths.

Confidence Maneuvers? Really a misnomer, I think, for they are really conceit shrinkers and consist of letting the plane pretty much fly itself to convince a skittish student that he is aboard a reliable, steady going craft that will treat him right if he'll give it a chance.

Coordination Exercises are a slow rocking of the plane to waltz time as a foundation for the so essential senses of timing and proper control pressures.

Climbs and Climbing Turns? Just learning to climb properly—too steep on your fluid air mass and you backslide—too shallow and you don't get anywhere.

Glides and Gliding Turns take you back down again—too steep and you're going too fast for a landing—too shallow and your speed slows to the point where your wings can't support your weight.

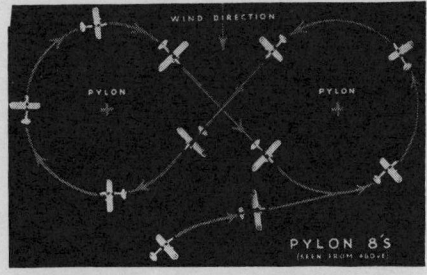

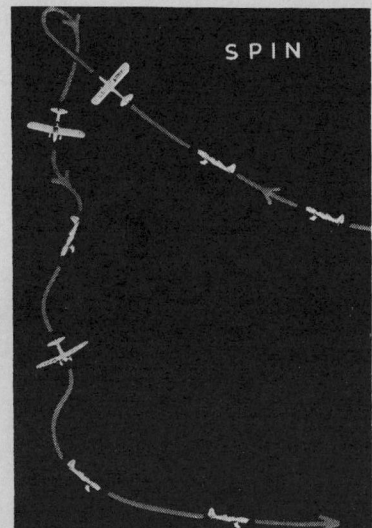

Having logged my 65 hours, I'll sign off, but not without a sincere thought of thanks to my instructors at the Ryan School of Aeronautics. Day in and day out with always the vista of another gang of Dodos just around the corner, they keep up a steady patience, interest and an undiminishing effort to grow wings on our clumsy shoulders.

When we're "down" they pick us up with a laconic word or two, or a verbal pat on the back. When we're too far up, they just as quietly haul us down to safe limits. Looking back, I know they've painstakingly, bit by bit, readied me for my three months at Randolph Field.

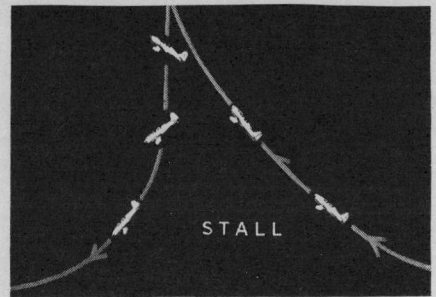

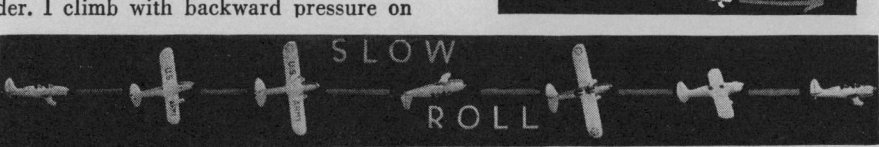

AERO DIGEST, April 1940

RYAN S-C
World's Finest Metal Cabin Plane for the Private Owner

WITH its modern metal construction, distinguished appearance and vision never before available in any cabin plane, the new three-place Ryan S-C is the outstanding plane in the private business and pleasure class.

Beautiful to look at, beautiful to handle, all who have seen and flown the S-C agree that it combines more advanced features than any other plane in its field.

MODERN DESIGN. The only truly modern design in its class now in production in America, the S-C has commanded the attention and enthusiasm of airwise pilots, operators and dealers wherever shown. The Ryan S-C is the first medium-weight cabin airplane that in design, engineering and manufacture takes full advantage of modern, all-metal construction and full cantilever low-wing streamlined efficiency.

Powered with a 145 h.p. Warner Super-Scarab radial engine, the S-C has a top speed of 150 m.p.h. and cruises comfortably at 135 m.p.h. The S-C takes off quicker and outclimbs any other plane in its class.

CONSTRUCTION. Ryan S-C fuselage, wings and other structural members are built of large, sturdy component metal parts. Greater simplicity—made possible by the Ryan precision die process of producing metal parts — means greater durability, lower maintenance cost and manufacturing economy. The sharply tapered, full cantilever wing structure is of the most advanced type, having Ryan patented features, a metal monospar and stressed skin metal front section. The full monocoque fuselage employs a thick gauge Alclad skin. Tail group and ailerons are metal structured of Alclad and steel, and are fabric covered. A single perforated flap is hinged on the under side of the wing between landing gear struts. The wide tread landing gear is of the single strut, full cantilever type completely faired.

A convertible type of airplane, the S-C has an ingeniously designed cabin hatch of flexible glass, that operates on roller bearings. By far, it is the easiest plane in its class to enter or leave.

The S-C is equipped with a single perforated landing flap hinged on the fuselage between legs of the landing gear.

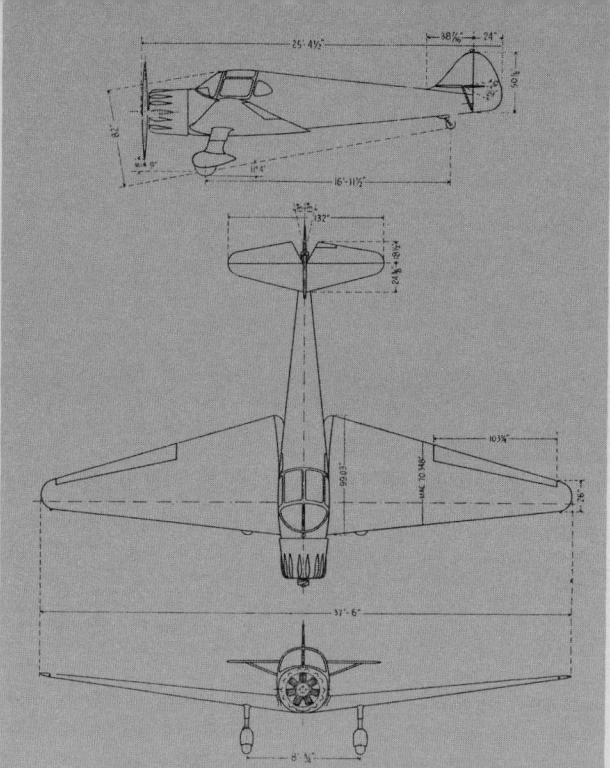

S-C OFFERS UNEXCELLED VISION

THE S-C possesses pilot and passenger vision that sets entirely new standards of excellence. The sliding cabin hatch, forward position of pilot, and low mounting of engine provide wide and unobstructed outlook upward, backward, in any degree of a banked turn, forward and downward.

Safe to fly, safe to land, the S-C is practically impossible to stall, and maintains full control in every maneuver. When forced into a spin, it possesses excellent spin characteristics, and recovery is immediate when controls are neutralized. The landing flap, long fuselage, wide landing gear and wheel brakes make the plane exceptionally easy to handle on landing and while rolling and taxiing.

For luxurious comfort the Ryan S-C offers a roomy cabin upholstered in fine grain leather. Pilot and one passenger sit side by side, with the third occupant accommodated in the wide rear seat. The cabin is heated, ventilated and soundproofed. The S-C has eye appeal plus, with its sharply tapered cantilever low wing, molded windshield and hatch, streamlined fuselage and fully faired landing gear.

PERFORMANCE AND SPECIFICATIONS

	SC-145
T.C. Number	658
Engine	Warner Super-Scarab
Horsepower	145 h.p. at 2050 rpm.
Maximum speed	150 m.p.h.
Cruising speed	135 m.p.h.
Landing speed with flaps	45 m.p.h.
Rate of climb	900 ft. per min.
Service ceiling	17,200 feet
Weight empty (average)	1345 lbs.
Useful load	805 lbs.
Pay load	390 lbs.
Gross weight	2150 lbs.
Cruising Range	500 miles
Wing loading	10.65 lbs./sq.ft.
Power loading	14.8 lbs./h.p.
Wing Span	37' 6"
Length Overall	25' 5 1/8"
Height Overall	7'
Wing Area (Inc. ailerons)	202 sq. ft.
Wheel tread	96 3/4"
Tire size	18x8-3 HD
Fuel Capacity	37 gals.
Oil Capacity	3 gals.

EQUIPMENT

The large useful load of the S-C allows for its generous standard equipment, including electric starter, battery, wheel pants, full fairing, split flap, deluxe interior finish, including ash trays, dome light, arm rests for all, adjustable pilot's seat, cabin heater, cool air ventilation system, concealed carburetor heater, stainless steel (non-rusting) exhaust manifold, retracting assist handles for easy entrance and other features usually classed as extras. The standard instrument group, supported on rubber mounts, includes: Altimeter, air speed indicator, tachometer, compass, oil pressure gauge and oil temperature gauge.

FOREIGN SHIPMENT

Ryan S-Cs for foreign shipment are wrapped and placed in a large box lined with waterproofing materials as an added preventative against salt water exposure. Wings and tail surfaces are disassembled, and the plane and engine placed in one box of the following approximate dimensions:

	English	Metric
Length	24' 2"	7.36 M.
Width	4' 8"	1.42 M.
Height	9' 6"	2.90 M.
Total Weight	4500 lbs.	2040 Kg.
Total Content	1070 cu. ft.	37.8 M3

The wide tread landing gear of the S-C is of the single strut, full cantilever type, completely faired.

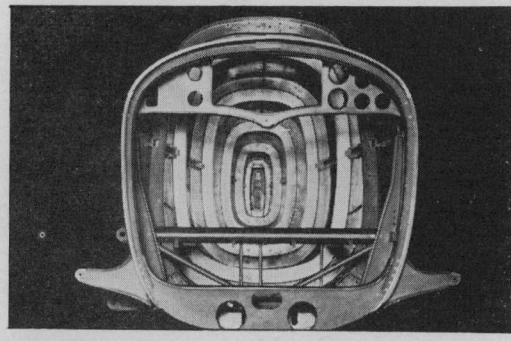

The S-C fuselage is of simplified, all metal, full monocoque construction using a thick gauge Alclad skin.

Note how the pilot may see over the engine cowling even when the plane is in taxiing position.

RYAN AERONAUTICAL COMPANY
LINDBERGH FIELD, SAN DIEGO, CALIFORNIA

Cable Address: "RYANCO"

Excerpted from SMILIN' JACK by Zack Mosley — 1938

Ryan ST-3

With the proud heritage of tens of thousands of hours in the hardest service to which airplanes can be subjected, the ST-3 is the crowning achievement in a long line of low wing trainers. With a longer and wider fuselage accentuating Ryan sleek lines the ST-3 abounds in engineering and structural refinements. Offered in a wider range of engines (2 radials and 2 in-lines from 125 to 160 h.p.) the ST-3 sets new standards of operating and training efficiency.

RYAN AERONAUTICAL COMPANY, Lindbergh Field, San Diego, California

RYAN TRAINERS ARE IN VOLUME PRODUCTION FOR U. S. ARMY AIR CORPS AND U. S. NAVY

See the New RYAN S-C at the CHICAGO SHOW
JAN. 28 to FEB. 6, 1938

In this remarkable new three-place cabin job you'll find more advanced features than any other plane in its field...modern metal construction...vision from every angle, never before approached in a closed ship... maneuverability and response to the controls that set a new high. It is the most roomy, comfortable and beautifully finished plane in its class. With a top speed of 150 m.p.h. and by far the slowest landing of any comparable plane, the Ryan S-C cruises comfortably at 135 m.p.h. Available with Warner Super Scarab 145 h.p. radial engine or Menasco 150 h.p. supercharged engine. Some choice dealerships will be allotted during the show. Your territory may be open. Investigate.

RYAN AERONAUTICAL CO.
Lindbergh Field, San Diego, California

S-T The Ryan Sport Trainer has won a universal acceptance never before attained in its field. New 1938 model with scores of improvements will be shown at Chicago.

SPORTSMAN PILOT, January 15, 1938

Available for DEMONSTRATION
RYAN'S Popular...
CABIN S-C W145 and OPEN S-T-A

Write or Phone
DEMORR AERONAUTICAL CORP.
Distributors for Eastern Pennsylvania, Southern New Jersey and Delaware
MAIN LINE AIRPORT
PAOLI — Tel. Paoli 1987 — PENNA.

SPORTSMAN PILOT, July 15, 1938

Flight Commanders to Dodos Know
RYAN BUILDS WELL!

CONFIDENCE for the student pilot, incentive for the instructor, comforting assurance for those at home—all result from the knowledge that Ryan builds airplanes well. In the services of the U. S. Army, U. S. Navy and United Nations, Ryan Primary Trainers are daily proving to be the world's finest. Vital as trainers are to achieving victory, building them well and in volume has been only part of important Ryan war assignments.

RELY ON Ryan TO BUILD WELL

RYAN AERONAUTICAL COMPANY, SAN DIEGO, CALIF.
Member, Aircraft War Production Council, Inc.
Ryan Products: Army PT-22s, Navy NR-1s, Army PT-25s, Major Sub-Assemblies and Exhaust Manifold Systems for America's Most Distinguished Aircraft

HERE'S WHY THE RUGGED, ALL-METAL RYAN NAVION GIVES YOU A GREATER MARGIN OF SAFETY!

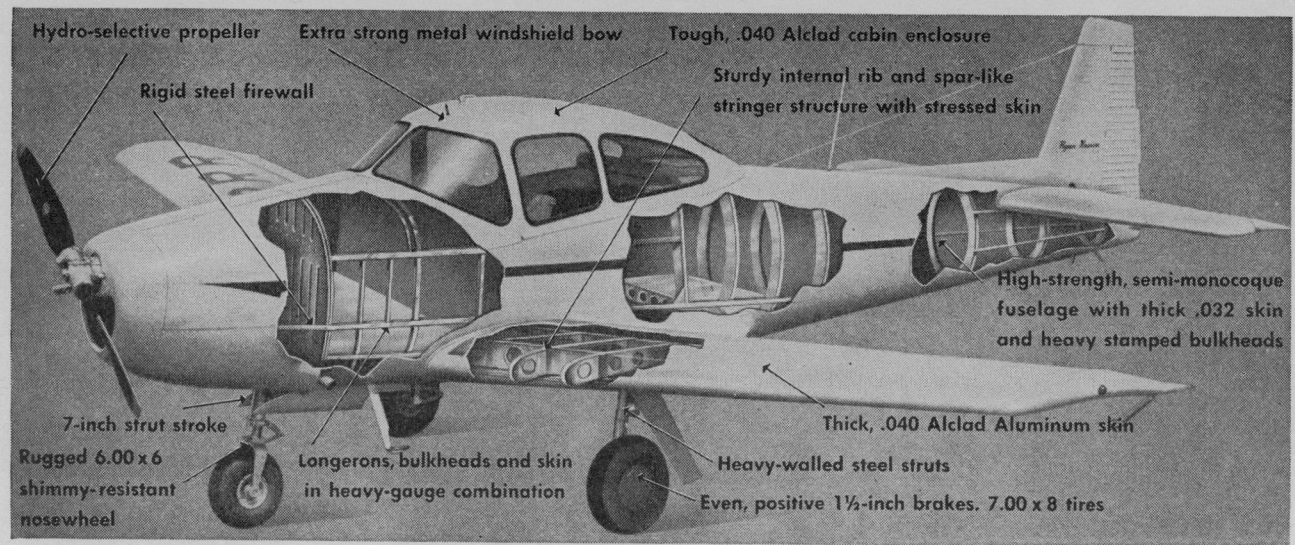

IT'S REALLY AS SIMPLE AS THIS: *Navion* is designed to be a safe, easy-to-fly plane. Within this fundamental premise, all other features are developed to the highest point *possible*. Navion is big and fast. It is rugged as a mule, and as hard-working. Aerodynamically and structurally it is designed, and is built, to take heavy-duty punishment. But, above all, the *Ryan Navion* is safe...and it is easy to fly. That's why it's first choice with non-professionals who fly for fun and profit. And, here's what makes it that way...

HUSKY, 205 h.p. engine features dual fuel system for dependability...delivers up to 155 m.p.h. cruising. Fully loaded, initial rate of climb is 900 ft. per minute.

SELECTIVE SETTING, high-lift flaps enable *Navion* to land at only 54 m.p.h. Only 875 ft. needed to clear a 50-ft. obstacle, either on take-off or landing...fully loaded, no wind.

NAVION GIVES YOU new VHF radio transmitter. Standard instruments now include manifold pressure, dampened fuel, outside temperature gauges, rate of climb indicator.

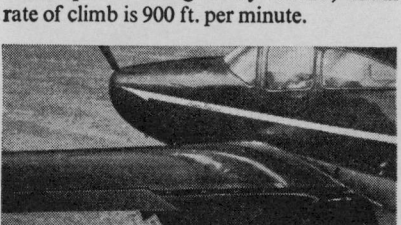

HERE'S THE FAMOUS *Navion* wing with its anti-stall design. For extra safety, full aileron control is yours even *below* stalling speed. Note full (43°) flap deflection.

THESE HEAVYWEIGHTS will take a beating! Big, steerable nosewheel is heavier than most "main" gears. Oversize tires; deep-stroke shocks for safe, easy rough-field landings.

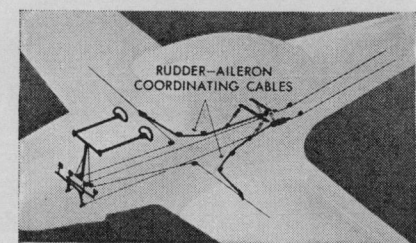

EXCLUSIVE rudder-aileron control linkage makes *Navion* so easy to fly. You get "two-control" after take-off, yet you have rudder when you want it. Write for FREE booklet.

Ryan Navion
NO OTHER PLANE COMBINES SO MANY FEATURES SO WELL

THESE COMFORT FEATURES ARE STANDARD EQUIPMENT
- "All-Round" Sound Insulation and Muffler
- Soft-Cushioned 43-in. Rear Seat
- Front Seats Adjust Individually
- New Heating-Ventilating System
- Limousine-Type Center Arm Rest
- In-Flight Access to Luggage
- Easy-Entrance Roll-Back Canopy

Rely on Ryan RYAN AERONAUTICAL COMPANY, 208 LINDBERGH FIELD, SAN DIEGO 12, CALIFORNIA

$9485.00
F.A.F. SAN DIEGO

NAVION UTILITY 205

Big—Rugged—Fast—Easy-to-Fly Safely—A Navion through and through

HERE'S THE MOST terrific value in aviation today...a tough 'n rugged 205 horsepower *Navion* for *only* $9485. A complete, well equipped plane, built for hard work. It's especially designed for business men, ranchers, contractors, oil men, star mail route operators and others who want modern, safe, fast air transportation at minimum cost. It features the same all-metal ruggedness as more expensive models...the same safety and ease-of-flying...the same VHF radio...the same kind of sensational performance on short, rough or muddy fields...*plus* large cargo space and greater payload. If an "air workhorse" can help you in *your* business, see the *Navion* Utility 205!

Ryan Navion

NO OTHER PLANE COMBINES SO MANY FEATURES SO WELL

IT'S EASY FOR ANYONE TO FLY A NAVION SAFELY! AND THERE'S A NAVION FOR EVERYONE!

‹ NAVION UTILITY 205. Features the proven *Navion* airframe and 205 hp Continental engine. Equipped with all essential accessories; others available at extra cost. 1029-lb. payload with full tanks, 55 cu. ft. cargo space.

‹‹ NAVION DELUXE 205. New, refined 1950 version of the plane that's made safe-flying history! In three striking new colors. Features new adjustable cowl flaps and cylinder-head temperature gauge, and more efficient radio antennae.

‹‹‹ NAVION SUPER 260. Lycoming-powered 260 hp. Cruises at an honest 170 mph. Takes off in 400 ft., climbs 1250 fpm. Has a service ceiling of 18,000 ft. Lands *under* 55 mph. Write today for more information on any or all new *Navions*.

Rely on Ryan **RYAN AERONAUTICAL COMPANY, 206 LINDBERGH FIELD, SAN DIEGO, CALIFORNIA**

RYAN VERTIJET!®

A *Major* Technical Breakthrough!

NOW IT CAN BE TOLD!

For many months Ryan X-13 pure jet VTOL research planes have been

1. Taking off vertically on jet thrust
2. Hovering stationary — maneuvering backward and sideways
3. Making the transition from vertical to horizontal flight — and back to vertical — with ease and precision
4. Flying as conventional delta-wing airplanes
5. Landing vertically

These are history-making accomplishments of major significance in world aeronautical progress. They culminate years of pioneering development by Ryan in the closest technical cooperation with the U.S. Air Force and the U.S. Navy.

By doing the heretofore impossible, Ryan Vertijets point toward an entirely new generation of jet aircraft of increasing capability — in climb, speed and altitude performance.

Those with vision can readily see where this milestone in the science of flight can lead. Ever increasing knowledge of jet VTOL is being unlocked by Ryan and the military services.

The Ryan X-13 Vertijet takes off and lands on a mobile ground service trailer, which can be moved from place to place to meet varying operating conditions. This new system of operation can release high-performance aircraft from dependence upon preparing airports and runways, vulnerable to destruction in time of conflict.

BUILDING AVIATION PROGRESS SINCE 1922

Aircraft • Power Plants • Avionics

Ryan Aeronautical Company, San Diego, Calif.
® REGISTERED TRADEMARK

Ryan Vertijet Brochure, 1957

EARLY RYAN AIRPLANES

THE FIRST RYAN cabin planes were converted Standard J-1 biplanes which were surplus World War I trainers. They were originally set up for two passengers in the front cockpit, and a pilot in the rear cockpit. The Ryan converted cabin accommodated four passengers after it had been widened six inches. Extra room was needed for passengers, so the fuselage gas tank was removed and mounted on top of the center section of the upper wing. Then the 100 hp Hall-Scott engine was replaced with a 150 hp Hispano-Suiza. Carrying a full load, the converted ships were faster than the original.

The Standards were operated mostly for sightseeing, and later on the Los Angeles-San Diego Air Line. Each plane differed in the changes made to the airframe. Ryan assigned aircraft numbers to each plane and named them. No. 6 was a narrow fuselage Standard named "Oneota", No. 8, with a fuselage and oval windows, was named "Palomar" and No. 10, with oval windows, was called "Miramar" and later became "El Condor Del Rio Mayo". These numbers ran from No. 1 through No. 10, the other planes being mostly **Jennies with one Thomas-Morse Scout (No. 5) and one Douglas Cloudster (No. 9).**

The sightseeing business was very successful, and it was this end of the business that held the school, and later the air line and factory together.

A Douglas Cloudster, Douglas (c/n 1), became Ryan conversion No. 9. The plane carried ten passengers besides the crew which is a very heavy load for one 400 hp Liberty engine. T. Claude Ryan had put her on her back at Los Angeles, after gliding too fast and overrunning the runway. None of the passengers were hurt, and the Cloudster was rebuilt and modified from its original open cockpit configuration to a cabin plane. At this time in 1926, the company was known as Ryan Airlines, Inc., even though it was not incorporated.

The Cloudster became the flagship of the Ryan fleet, and was used in the airline and for charter. Heavy rains in late 1926 had washed out the roads between Mexicali and Tijuana stopping the shipment of beer between the two towns. The Cloudster was used to haul beer in barrels for two or three months until the road was repaired.

A charter was arranged that would bring her back to San Diego via Ensenada. The problem was that Ensenada had no airfield. You were supposed to land on the beach when the tide was out. Red Harrigan, the pilot, landed on the beach, only the tide was in. The plane turned over on its back in shallow water, fortunately hurting no one. It was night by this time, and a rope was secured to the propeller so the Cloudster would not float away. The next morning, with adequate manpower to move the plane, it was found that she had disintegrated during the night, and all that was still attached to the rope was a Liberty engine.

BIRTH OF THE M-1

The first freehand sketches of the Ryan Airlines M-1 were made in the fall of 1925. The idea was to have a high wing monoplane with open cockpits. This would present less drag than a biplane, give better visibility and use a smaller engine. The design called for a cruise speed of 115 mph, and a six hundred pound payload of passengers and mail.

Under the direction of Ryan, John van der Linde and Hawley Bowlus built the first M-1 (M for monoplane, and 1 for the first series). She was an externally braced, high wing parasol with a span of 36 ft, and two open cockpits. The wings were fabric covered with wooden ribs and plywood full span box spars. The airfoil was a Clark "Y" and the wing was internally wire braced. The fuselage was fabric covered with a steel tubing frame of a Z braced box type. One feature that almost could be called a trade mark found on all Ryan cabin planes was the "jeweling" or "engine turning" achieved by burnishing the aluminum cowl and wheel covers.

With the help of John K. Northrop, the plane had some refinements and changes made. The most important was the switch from the box spar wing to an "I-beam" wing which reduced the weight by 200 lbs. The Hisso water radiator was moved from the wing leading edge where it interfered with the air flow, to under the fuselage. The Hisso engine was the logical choice for the first M-1 for it was an available and inexpensive surplus power plant.

Nine M-1 aircraft were built before the improved wing was used. The most common engine was the Wright 200 hp J-4B. Other tested were the Curtiss 90 hp OX-5, LeRhone 110 and 120 hp and the 150 Hisso.

The first M-1 was tested carrying a payload of 500 lb., which it did easily. Vern C. Gorst needed aircraft for the Pacific Air Transport, an airmail route along the West Coast, and was interested in the M-1. It was his suggestion to

substitute the Wright J-4B for the Hispano. M-1 serial c/n 2 was built with the Wright engine, and in March, just a month after its test flight, it was flown from Los Angeles to Seattle, but not without incident. No Ryan M-1 or M-2 aircraft had wheel brakes and landing at Fresno, Ryan and Gorst were unable to stop at the end of the short runway, and damaged the landing gear. With the gear repaired, the flight was continued to San Francisco. The flight from San Francisco to Seattle was flown in a record time of seven hours and three minutes.

The M-1 was attracting a great deal of attention by this time, and when Ryan made a landing at Pearson Field, Vancouver, Washington on his return from Seattle, a race was agreed on between the M-1 and an Army De Havilland. The De Havilland was a two-place 400 hp biplane used to carry mail, and was considered the fastest the Air Corps had. On the surface it seemed an unfair race — a 200 hp M-1 against a 400 hp Army plane to be piloted by the famed Lt. Oakley Kelly. The race was to be a gentlemanly three laps around a 2½ mile course. The resulting competition was anything but friendly, and had a lasting effect on the fortunes of the Ryan Co.

The De Havilland lost badly. Lt. Kelly took it like a gentlemen, but the Army did not. They were embarrassed, and it was almost 12 years before Ryan got a government contract.

But the race helped clinch the deal with Vern Gorst, and he ordered six M-1 aircraft with Wright engines. They were priced at $2 400 each for a total of $14,400, and the engines were an additional price of $5000 each. At a later date, Gorst's Pacific Air Transport ordered two more for a total of eight. It was nearly six months before P.A.T. started service, and during this time M-1 (c/n 3 NC-1225) was flown by Vance Breese in a number of competitions and exhibitions.

In August, 1926, Breese flew the M-1 in the Mile High Air Meet at Denver, and won three first place trophies, including the Grand Sweepstakes for the best all-around performance. Again in late August with the M-1 now marked with a large 23, she was flown in the Ford Reliability Tour. The demonstration flights and aerobatics were spectacularly performed by Breese, and in the formal part of this second Ford Tour, he placed eighth.

M-1 (c/n 3) made her last flight October 26, 1927 with C. R. (Dick) Bowman of P.A.T. at the controls. He bailed out at 9000 ft over the Techachapi Mountains after his carburetor and wings iced up. He was alright but was a week later before they found the remains of the M-1.

M-1 (c/n 5, NC-2070) got into trouble shortly after take off from Los Angeles. The pilot, Charles Widmer, got into the clouds and lost control. He parachuted to safety, but unfortunately the passenger, Shorty Rossitter, was killed when the plane crashed in the Hollywood Mountains. Rossitter had a parachute, but was unable to get out, being in the front cockpit up under the wing.

Another P.A.T. M-1 (c/n 8, NC-2073) piloted by Eddie Neher crashed in a storm front near Gustine, west of Fresno.

Five of the first M-1's bought by P.A.T. crashed during the first year, mainly because of inadequate airway aids and bad weather. By 1928, the Ryan M-1's had all been phased out and sold.

One M-1 buyer was Ernest L. Smith, an early pilot for P.A.T. In July, 1927, he and Emory B. Bronte became the first civilians to fly from California to Hawaii in the Travel Air "City of Oakland".

Frank Wiley, a former Ryan Airlines pilot, took delivery of M-1 (c/n 23, NC-2532) on March, 1927, and flew the plane to Scobey, Montana for the Westland Oil Co. The M-1 was then modified with an enclosed cabin, and was on the CAA register as an M-1C, Hisso powered. This aircraft is now the sole remaining M-1 in existence, and is on permanent display in the San Diego Aero Space Museum.

One special M-1 (c/n 10, NC-3219) was fitted with a cabin at the factory and it was modified so much it became the "Bluebird" and not just an M-1. The pilots seat was moved to the front from the usual rear seat position. She was the first I-beam spar 36 ft Northrop designed wing. The engine was a Wright manufactured Hispano-Suiza E-2 V8 of 200 hp. Other features were a cabin door on the right side, and a color scheme that led to the name "Bluebird". The flying characteristics were about the same as for an equally powered M-1 or M-2, but she had a somewhat hotter landing speed.

It was at this time, November, 1926, that T. Claude Ryan sold his interest in the company to his partner, B. Franklin Mahoney.

A tall young man visited Ryan Field in February, 1927 and test flew a Hisso powered M-1. There was little doubt in anyone's mind after his low altitude stunt flying that afternoon that this man could really handle an airplane. He wanted a special plane similar to the five place cabin ship partly built in the Ryan shop, but one with a 46 ft wing instead of the 42 ft planned for the new Brougham, and the pilot in the rear so extra gas tanks could be centered under the wing.

Donald Hall and Charles Lindbergh with the help of 20 factory workers under Hawley Bowlus built the N.Y.P. (New York-Paris) in sixty days after actual construction was started. This could not have been done this fast if it had not been for the work and engineering that had gone into the construction of the first B model Brougham cabin plane. Lindbergh provided two super inspected Wright J-5C engines, the first of which was damaged slightly so the second was used. The airframe cost Lindbergh and his St. Louis backers $10,580, including mounting the engine, but excluding the cost of the engines themselves.

The first test flight was very spectacular, as just after take off a Navy pursuit turned in and tried to follow the "Spirit", but was outclassed at every maneuver. Seven test flights, including those with 36 gals., 71, 111, 151, 201, 251 and 301 gallons of fuel and 4 gallons of oil, were carried out at Camp Kearney over the next few weeks. The Spirit of St. Louis left San Diego on May 10, 1927. The rest is history.

Because of Lindbergh's flight to Paris in a Ryan monoplane, the factory received more orders than it could fill. The number of workers increased from 20 to 120, and the new B-1 cabin planes were being built and sold at a rate of almost 3 a week.

The first B (c/n 31, NC-3007) completed was a B.2 powered by a Hisso engine. The second was a B.1 (c/n 29, NC-3009) with a Wright J-5 Whirlwind. Number 29 had been under construction when the NYP was ordered, but work was stopped on this B.1 ordered originally by Dick Robinson and resumed *after* the completion of the N.Y.P. Ultimately Frank Hawks took delivery of c/n 29 and named her "Gold Bug" and flew her in the 1927 Ford Reliability Tour as number 22 and placed eighth. Still later it was renamed "Pride of San Diego".

The factory has no information on the difference between B.1 and B.2 aircraft. The first B model manufactured did have a Hisso engine, and was factory designated a B.2; later it was re-engined with a Wright J-5B, and then carried on the CAA register as a B.1. The engine, it seems to me, in all likelihood was the model difference. Only three Hisso powered B models were manufactured.

There is considerable differences in the tail shape and size between early and late B.1's. They were built with different windshield shapes and with tail skids and tailwheels, with two cabin doors or one cabin door. The early models had large fairings over rubber shock cords on the

landing gear, but the late ships were Aerol (air-oil) with small fairings. However, the general construction of all the "Brougham" series was very similar. They had welded chrome-moly steel tubing frame faired to shape and covered with fabric. Their cabins were luxuriously appointed, and were insulated against noise and temperature. The wing had an I-beam solid spruce spar, with wood ribs and plywood gussets and was fabric covered.

The second B.1 (c/n 32, NC-3113), was piloted and partly owned by A. D. Cruickshank, a district representative of the northwest Mounted Police. Her registry was changed to G-CAHR, and she was one of the pioneer bush planes, operating on skis and wheels in Canada and Alaska.

Number 48 was the first Ryan to fly with full technical data, and to receive an Aircraft Type Certificate. Like many manufacturers of that day, no one at the Mahoney factory had run stress analysis on any B.1 aircraft. Approved Type Certificate number 25 was issued January, 1928 on B.1's. Number 48 became NS-15 on delivery to Clarence M. Young, head of the Aeronautics Branch of the Department of Commerce.

Ryan B.1 (c/n 143) made a number of long distance flights over a total of 3600 miles from Canton to Mukden, Manchuria, then on to Naching. The pilot was General Chang Wei-Chang who was later named Director of Aviation of the Chinese War Department.

The Mahoney-Ryan model B.3 was a typical "Brougham" with very few differences from the previous design. She was available with a Wright J-5C of 220 hp, or a Wright J-6-9 of 300 hp. The three most visible changes were: a rudder that was not counterbalanced, ailerons that were inset in the wings and did not extend to the tips, and last, when the J-6-9 engine was used, no spinner due to a front exhaust collector. ATC 104 was issued in January, 1929, and amended under Group 2 approval number 2-50 in March to cover three B.3's with Wright J-6-9 300 hp engines.

Ryan B.1 serial (c/n 52, NC-1766) was not a new aircraft when Reginald Robbins and James Kelly set an airborne endurance record. They kept the Brougham aloft for six days, refueling air-to-air twice a day. Only because of a mechanical problem in the form of a split propeller did they land after 172 hours and 32 minutes. As a reward, they were given a new Ryan B.3 (c/n 184, NC-7736) and collected $50,000 in prize money.

Marvel Crosson a 20 year old aviatrix used a Ryan B.3 (c/n 185, NC-7737) to make an altitude record for women. She took off from Los Angeles and climbed to 23,996 ft which bested the old mark by 3726 ft.

The Ryan B.5, ATC 142 (June 13, 1929) was powered only by the Wright J-6-9 300 hp engine. She was very similar to the B.3 with a J-6-9 engine. The only visible distinctive feature to differentiate the two were: a decorative wide stripe under the cabin windows, a more prominent radius on the side windshield panels, and a slightly more rounded vertical fin. More and more planes were purchased by big businesses; a few examples are Prest-O-Lite, Pampa Refineries, Pikes Peak Air Lines and the Fort Wayne Sentinel. Two were fitted with floats by the Land of Lakes Airways Corp., and were flown by the St. John's Military Academy.

A B.5 was flown by Russell Young in the National Air Tour for 1929, and placed 19th among a large number of competitors.

Approximately 22 of the 61 B.5's produced flew with Mexican licenses. Seven B.1's and two B.3's had previously gone to Mexico.

Pickwick Latin American Airways inaugurated a three-flight-a-week mail and passenger service over the 2700 mile route between Los Angeles and Guatemala via Mexico City. The trips were a series of daylight flights with stopovers at Nogales and Mazatlan.

Wuhan Civil Aviation Association bought five B.5's for a scheduled service between Hankow and Canton, China. Two China B.5 Ryans were operated on floats.

The Ryan model B 7 was an enlarged version of the previous model B.5. This model provided extra performance with a 9 cylinder Pratt & Whitney Wasp C-1 engine of 420 hp. Her appearance was basically the same but with a longer and fuller fuselage. The same elegance and appointments that were the trademark of earlier Broughams were very much in evidence. She was the end of this line for Ryan Broughams and the most advanced, quite an improvement in only 3 years from the first M-1 to the power and grace of the B 7 in 1929. Type Certificate 262 was issued October 26, 1929 for both land and seaplanes.

The "Foursome" or C 1 model Ryan was designed by Art Mankey and built in the St. Louis plant. On August 11, 1930, she received Approved Type Certificate 346.

This new cabin plane with seating for four was much smaller than her predecessors and was aimed at a different market. More of a sport plane or small family ship than the larger more powerful Broughams, she was built for wealthy private owners.

Powered with a 7 cylinder Wright J-6 (R-760) engine of 225 hp and later by the J-6-7 of 240 hp, only three aircraft were produced.

Originally 401 was modified as a model C 2 with a Packard Diesel DR-980. This engine installation was approved on Group 2 Certificate 2-263 on August 20, 1930. The aircraft was later converted to a Wright R-760 and redesignated C 1. She was purchased by the Horlick Malted Milk Co., and later acquired by Alexander Loeb and Richard Decker in 1938. After being fitted with extra fuel

tanks and named SHALOM, she was flown long distances for records. One attempted record was from New York to Palestine, but the plane blew a tire on take off and never made it off the ground. The last attempt at a record flight was from Point Michraup Beach, Nova Scotia on August 11, 1939 to Europe. It was an ill-fated flight, for they never arrived and no trace of them was ever found.

Number 402 was reportedly purchased by Vance Breese, and is now the only remaining C 1 in existence.

As late as 1962, six Ryan cabin planes remained on the FAA register. This list has been decimated by the movie industry and others making NYP replicas. In 1975, only one B.1, one C 1 and one M-1 remain.

— Dorr B. Carpenter

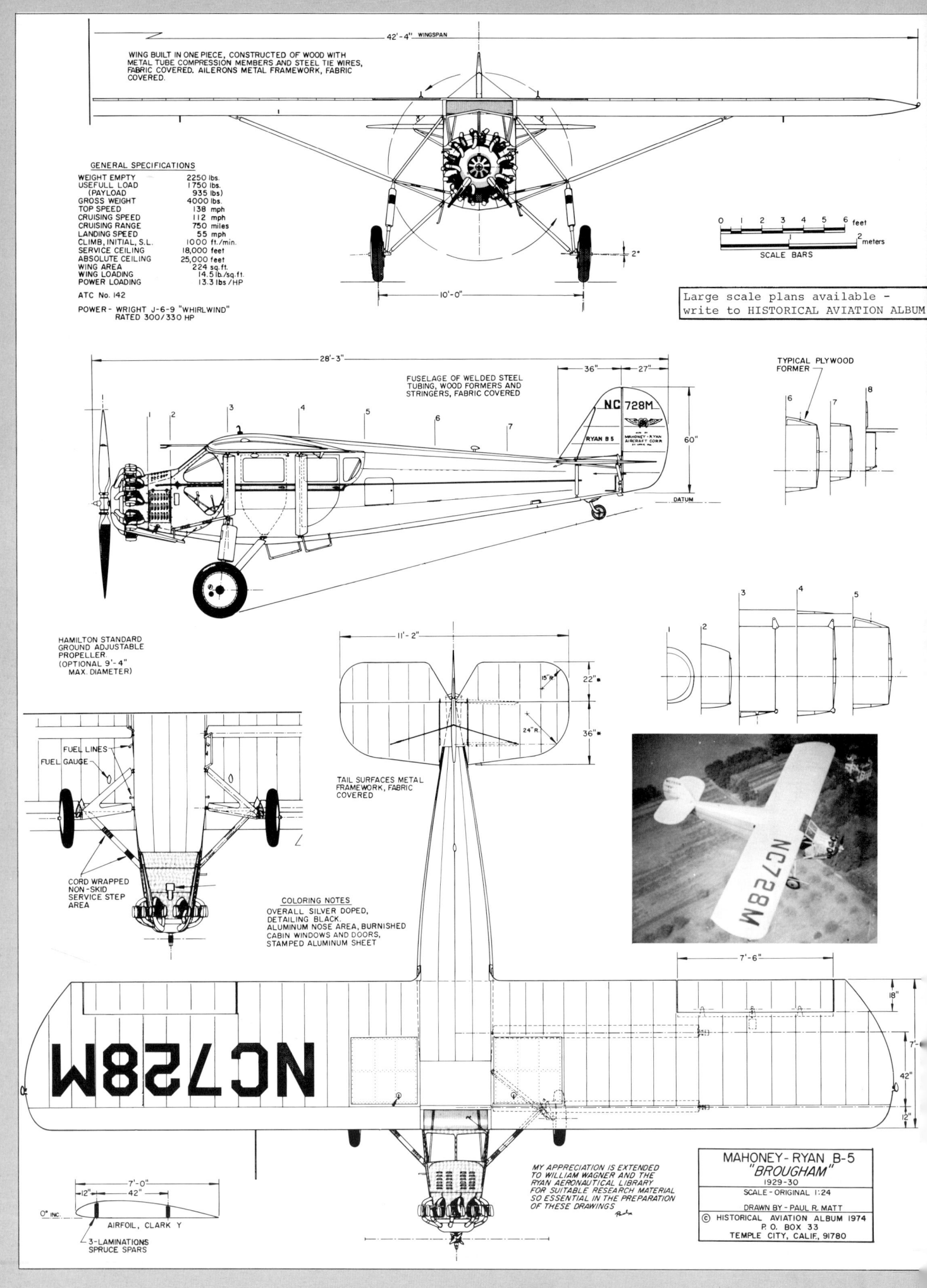

Ryan (Douglas) Cloudster as first used

B.5 c/n 247 CF-AWY -E. J. Bulban photo

The Bluebird NC3219 c/n 10 -Ryan

M-1 with J-4-B Whirlwind for Pacific Air

B.1 c/n 159 as N.Y.P. replica -Leo Kohn

B. 1 c/n 72 on floats (Mayborn)

M-1 with Whirlwind -Bill Larkins

M-2 c/n 24 as duster -John Underwood

M-2 identified as 3116 - ? c/n -Erickson

B.1 c/n 159 became N.Y.P. replica -L. Kohn

B.1 Special c/n 42 "MGM special"   -Ryan

B.1 on floats c/n 95 as NC-4941 -Leo Kohn

B.1 c/n 148 in Calcutta - 1928-Greg Kohn

B.1 c/n 32, 3113 became G-CAHR Canada

B.1 c/n 131 NC6646 after much use -L Kohn

B.1 Brougham   -Ryan photo (Erickson)

Early Ryans

c/n	Identification	Date	Model	Engine	Remarks
1	3252(?)	2-14-26	M-1	Hisso	
2	4041	-	M-1	J4B	Crash 12-25
3	NC-1225	-	M-1	J4B	PAT
4	2069	1926	M-1	J4B	PAT, Crash Fresno
5	2070	1926	M-1	J4B	PAT, Crash 11-26
6	2071	1926	M-1	J4	PAT #6
7	4327	1926	M-1	-	PAT #7
8	2073	1926	-	-	PAT #8, Crash
9	2068	1926	M-1	-	PAT
10	3219	1926	Bluebird	Hisso E	Crash/rebuilt M-2
11	3253(?)	-	M-2	-	-
12	-	-	-	-	-
13	-	-	-	-	-
14	2341(?)	-	M-2	-	-
15	1609	-	M-2	-	-
16	C-2345	1926	M-2C	Hisso E	-
17	-	-	-	-	-
18	3393	-	M-2	-	Crash 1928
19	X-1057	-	M-2	Hisso	-
20	C-10026	1927	M-3C	Hisso 180	Two c/n 20
20	1133	-	M-2	-	-
21	C-90	1927	M-2	Hisso 180	Two c/n 21
21	C-203	1926	M-1	Hisso 180	
22	2769	-	M-2	Hisso/J4	to G-CAJK
23	2532	3-19-27	M-3/M-1C	Hisso	Now in S.D. Museum
24	C-141E	1926	M-2	Ryan-Siem	Two c/n 24
24	4282	-	M-2		
25	C-2746	1927	M-2	Hisso 180	
26	C-1317	1927	M-2C	Hisso 150	
27	1779	-	M-2	Hisso	
28	C-909	7-17-27	M-2	Hisso 180	
29	2341	-	M-2	Ryan-Siem.	Two c/n 29
29	3009/1105	1927	B.1	J5	Hawk's Gold Bug
30	N-X-211	3-27-27	N.Y.P.	J5C	Spirit of St. Louis
31	C-3007	1927	B.2/B.1	Hisso/J5B	

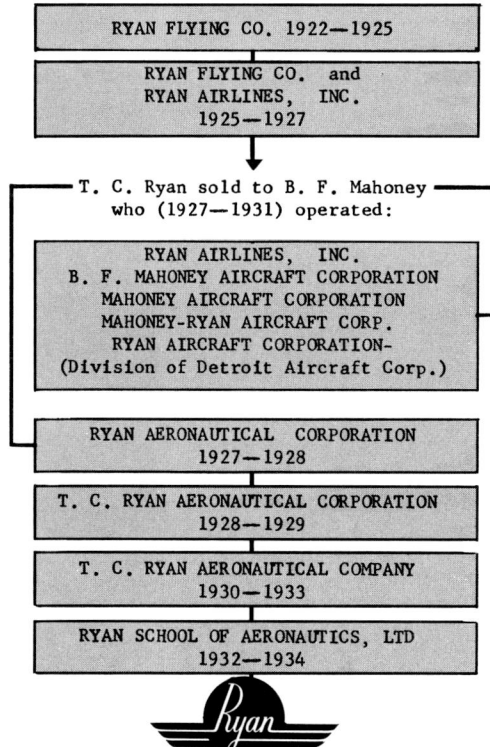

RYAN GENEOLOGY
(simplified)

RYAN FLYING CO. 1922—1925

RYAN FLYING CO. and RYAN AIRLINES, INC. 1925—1927

T. C. Ryan sold to B. F. Mahoney who (1927—1931) operated:

RYAN AIRLINES, INC.
B. F. MAHONEY AIRCRAFT CORPORATION
MAHONEY AIRCRAFT CORPORATION
MAHONEY-RYAN AIRCRAFT CORP.
RYAN AIRCRAFT CORPORATION-
(Division of Detroit Aircraft Corp.)

RYAN AERONAUTICAL CORPORATION 1927—1928

T. C. RYAN AERONAUTICAL CORPORATION 1928—1929

T. C. RYAN AERONAUTICAL COMPANY 1930—1933

RYAN SCHOOL OF AERONAUTICS, LTD 1932—1934

Ryan AERONAUTICAL COMPANY 1934—1968

TELEDYNE RYAN AERONAUTICAL
2701 HARBOR DRIVE • SAN DIEGO, CALIFORNIA 92112
1969—to present

B.1 Production

			(c/n 29 & 31 with Early Aircraft)
32	3113	1927	to G-CAHR (Canada)
33	NC-1225	-	-
34	C-1415	1927	-
35	C-866	1927	
36	J-BAAC	1927	NYP-2
37	C-958	1927	Robertson A/C
38	NC-1159	-	Cleveland Pneumatic
39	NC-3257	-	"Pride of Pittsburgh"
40	NC-1630	1927	SW Ryan Airline
41	C-1787	1927	VanHoffman
42	1550	-	MGM Special
43	-	-	-
44	C-1962	1927	-
45	NC-1986	-	-
46	NC-3226	1928	"The Betty Rogers"
47	G-AUNZ	-	To Australia
48	NS-15	1927	ATC 25 1-27-28
49	C-3598	1927	B.1-Special "Pot Bellied"
50	C-3422	-	to XA-BIB
51	NC-3423	-	Anheuser-Busch
52	C-1766	11-27	172½ hr endurance
53	C-3565	-	Capital Airways
54	C-3648	1927	
55	C-3775	1927	
56	C-3746	1927	to XA-BHD
57	C-3810	1927	Southwest Ryan AL
58	NC-3845	1927	
59	NC-3910	1927	
60	C-4094	1928	
61	C-9113	1928	With floats (no ATC)
62	4031	1927	
63	C-4034	1928	
64	NC-4087	-	
65	C-4089	1928	
66	C-4090	1928	
67	C-4135	1928	
68	NC-4467	-	
69	NX-4215	1928	B.1X Lindbergh Special
70	C-4333	1928	Scenic Airways

71	NC-4398	1928	
72	C-4474	1928	
73	NC-4459	1928	
74	C-4560	1928	
75	C-4561	1928	
76	NC-4562	1928	
77	C-4563	1928	
78	C-4653	1928	
79	NC-4654	3-28	later Braniff
80	4655	1928	
81	4656	1928	
82	NC-4657	1928	
83	NC-4658	1928	Seaboard Al.
84	C-4659	1928	"Pride of Susquehanna"
85	C-4931	1928	Continental Oil
86	C-4932	1928	
87	NC-4933	1928	
88	C-4934	1928	
89	C-4935	1928	
90	C-4936	1928	Texas Air Transport
91	NC-4937	1928	Albany Air Svc.
92	4938	1928	
93	4939	1928	
94	C-4940	1928	
95	C-4941	1928	
96	C-4942	1928	
97	C-5209	1928	
98	5210	1928	
99	C-5211	1928	Ev Cassagneres has remains
100	C-5212	1928	
101	C-5213	1928	
102	NC-5214	1928	
103	C-5215	1928	
104	NC-5216	1928	
105	C-5217	1928	
106	NC-5218	1928	
107	C-5219	1928	
108	C-5220	1928	Ev Cassagneres has remains
109	C-5544	1928	

Test flying the N.Y.P. -H A Erickson

The N.Y.P -H. A. "Jimmy" Erickson (Ryan)

Dirt field flying after Paris (Mayborn)

Ryan SPEEDSTER was really Parks P-2A and is not considered a Ryan today. -B. Hodges

C.1 c/n 401 with Alex Loeb -Gregory Kohn

B.5 with J-6-9 on floats -Leo Kohn

B.1 (called B.2 with Hisso engine -Ryan

M-1 c/n 1 and STA c/n 101 -Underwood

B.1 Production

#	Reg	Date	Notes
110	NC-5545	1928	to
111	C-5546	5-28-28	Dates are wing completion
112	5547	5-29-28	7th Place '28 Ford tour
113	5548	5-31-28	
114	C-5549	6-2-28	
115	C-5550	6-5-28	
116	C-5551	6-7-28	
117	C-5552	6-8-28	
118	C-5553	6-9-28	Flown in Pike's Peak Tour
119	C-5554	6-12-28	
120	C-5555	6-13-28	
121	NC-5556	6-14-28	
122	NC-5557	6-15-28	
123	C-5558	6-18-28	Crash near Chicago '28
124	NC-5559	6-19-28	
125	C-6583	6-21-28	
126	C-6584	6-22-28	
127	C-6585	6-26-28	
128	NC-6586	6-28-28	
129	NC-6587	6-29-28	Dallas Air Taxi
130	C-6645	6-29-28	
131	C-6646	7-2-28	
132	C-6647	7-5-28	
133	C-6648	7-6-28	
134	C-6649	7-9-28	Beacon Airways
135	C-6650	7-10-28	
136	C-6651	7-11-28	Crash 1-12-30
137	C-6652	7-13-28	
138	C-6653	7-14-28	
139	NC-6654	1928	on floats
140	NC-6955	1928	
141	C-6956	7-17-28	
142	6957	7-19-28	
143	6958	7-19-28	
144	C-6959	7-20-28	
145	6960	7-23-28	
146	6961	7-24-28	to Guatemala
147	C-6962	7-25-28	
148	6963	7-27-28	to G-AUIX Australia
149	7202	7-20-28	
150	C-7203	7-31-28	
151	NC-7204	8-1-28	
152	C-7205	8-3-28	
153	C-7206	8-11-28	NYP Replica by Paul Mantz
154	C-7207	8-21-28	
155	7208	8-22-82	
156	NC-7209	8-23-28	NYP Replica in Ford Museum
157	C-7210	8-24-28	
158	NC-7211	8-25-28	
159	NC-7212	8-29-28	NYP Replica in EAA Museum
160	C-7213	8-20-28	
161	C-7214	8-31-28	
162	7215	9-7-28	
163	C-7671	9-5-28	1st Plywood edge wing.
164	NC-7672	9-7-28	
165	NC-7673	9-11-28	
166	C-7674	9-12-28	
167	7719	9-14-28	to G-AAEK
168	7720	9-18-28	China ???
169	7721	9-18-28	"
170	7722	9-20-28	"
171	7723	9-24-28	"
172	7724	9-25-28	"
173	NC-7725	9-26-28	
174	NC-7726	9-27-28	to X-ABHE later X-BAHE
175	NC-7727	9-29-28	to X-ABHF
176	7728	10-1-28	to X-ABHG, crash Oct 26, 1929
177	7729	10-3-28	
178	7730	10-5-28	

End of B.1 production and San Diego Production

B.3 Production

#	Reg	Date	Notes
179	C-114E	10-9-28	J5B engine
180	NC-7732	10-11-28	J5B engine
181	NC-7733	10-19-28	to XB-AIA (J5)
182	NC-7734	-	J5 engine
183	7735	1929	R-975 at first
184	7736	1929	J6 engine
185	C-7737	1929	R-975 (Crosson)
186	NC-7738	1929	J6 engine

210 as B.3A in B.5 production list next.

B.5 Production

B.5 Brougham Production (except as noted)

#	Reg	Date	Notes
187	X-8321	1929	R-975 engine
188	NC-9230	1929	R-975
189	C-9231	1929	J6 (to CF-AEV)
190	C-9232	1929	Prest-O-Lite
191	NC-9233	1929	J-6
192	NC-9234	1929	J-6
193	C-9235	1929	J-6
194	NC-9236	1929	Last B.5 flying
195	C-9237	1929	J-6
196	NC-9238	1929	J-6
197	NC-9239	1929	J-6
198	NC-9240	1929	J-6
199	NC-14H	1929	J-6
200	NC-15H	1929	B.5A w/Wasp Jr.
201	NC-16H	1929	to X-ABFL
202	NC-17H	1929	J-6
202	NC-17H	1929	J-6
203	NC-18H	1929	
204	NC-8320	1929	J-6
205	NC-306K	1929	J-6
206	NC-307K	1929	J-6, to X-ABFF
207	NC-308K	1929	J-6
208	NC-309K	1929	to NC-128W
209	CF-AHD	1929	Yukon Airways
210	NC-311K	1929	B.3A, J-5 engine
211	NC-312K	1929	to NC-131W to X-ABFA
212	NC-313K	1929	to X-BAJF
213	NC-314K	1929	J-6 (to Mexico)
214	NC-315K	1929	J-6, to X-ABJN
215	NC-378K	1929	J-6
216	379K	1929	-
217	380K	1929	-
218	381K	8-27-29	J-6, to X-BADP
219	382K	1929	-
220	383K	1929	-
221	384K	1929	-
222	-	1929	-
223	310K	1929	-
224	741M	1929	to X-ABFD
225	NC-725M	1929	to X-ABFI
226	NC-132W	1929	NC-362K/X-ABFJ/X-ABAZ
227	727M	1929	-
228	NC-728M	1929	-
229	729M	1929	-
230	730M	1929	-
231	731M	1929	-
232	NC-732M	10-19-29	-
233	733M	-	-
234	734M	-	-
235	NC-735M	-	Robertson A/c
236	736M	-	-
237	737M	-	to X-ACAF
238	NC-738M	-	J-6-9, Robertson
239	NC-739M	-	Robertson, to X-ABAQ
240	740M	-	-
241	385K	-	-
242	550N	-	-
243	543N	-	-
244	544N	-	-
245	NC-545N	-	to X-ABDF
246	246Y	-	-
247	NC-12852	-	to CF-AWY
248	NC-8493	-	to CF-ANP to X-ACAQ

B7 Production

#	Reg	Date	Notes
249	NC-549M	10-26-29	Became X-ACEO
250	NC-555N	12- -29	Robertson Aircraft
251	NC-724M	-	-
252	NC-720M	-	-
253	NC-721M	-	-
254	-268Y	-	-
255	NC-723M	-	National Airlines (Memo 2-223)
256	-12822	-	-

B.5 c/n 190 NC9232 — Ryan

B.5 c/n 192 NC9234 — Gregory Kohn

B.1 c/n 52 record 172½ hrs — Greg Kohn

B.3 c/n 184 donated to Kelly & Robbins

B.5 c/n 238 NC738M — Burton Kemp

B.1 c/n 167 as G-AAEK — John Underwood

M-1 Wright J-4B at San Diego (Mayborn)

M-2 with Hisso - note difference (Mayborn)

B.3 with J-5C and jeweled cowl

B.1 fuselage - Z braced box type   -Ryan

B.1 Rudder outline-dotted early shape

B.1 elevator construction - late model

B.1 Cockpit - late model   -Ryan

B.5 cabin   -Ryan

T. C. Ryan Flying School (1929) B.1 c/n 93

Frank Hawk's B.1 "Gold Bug" (John Underwood)

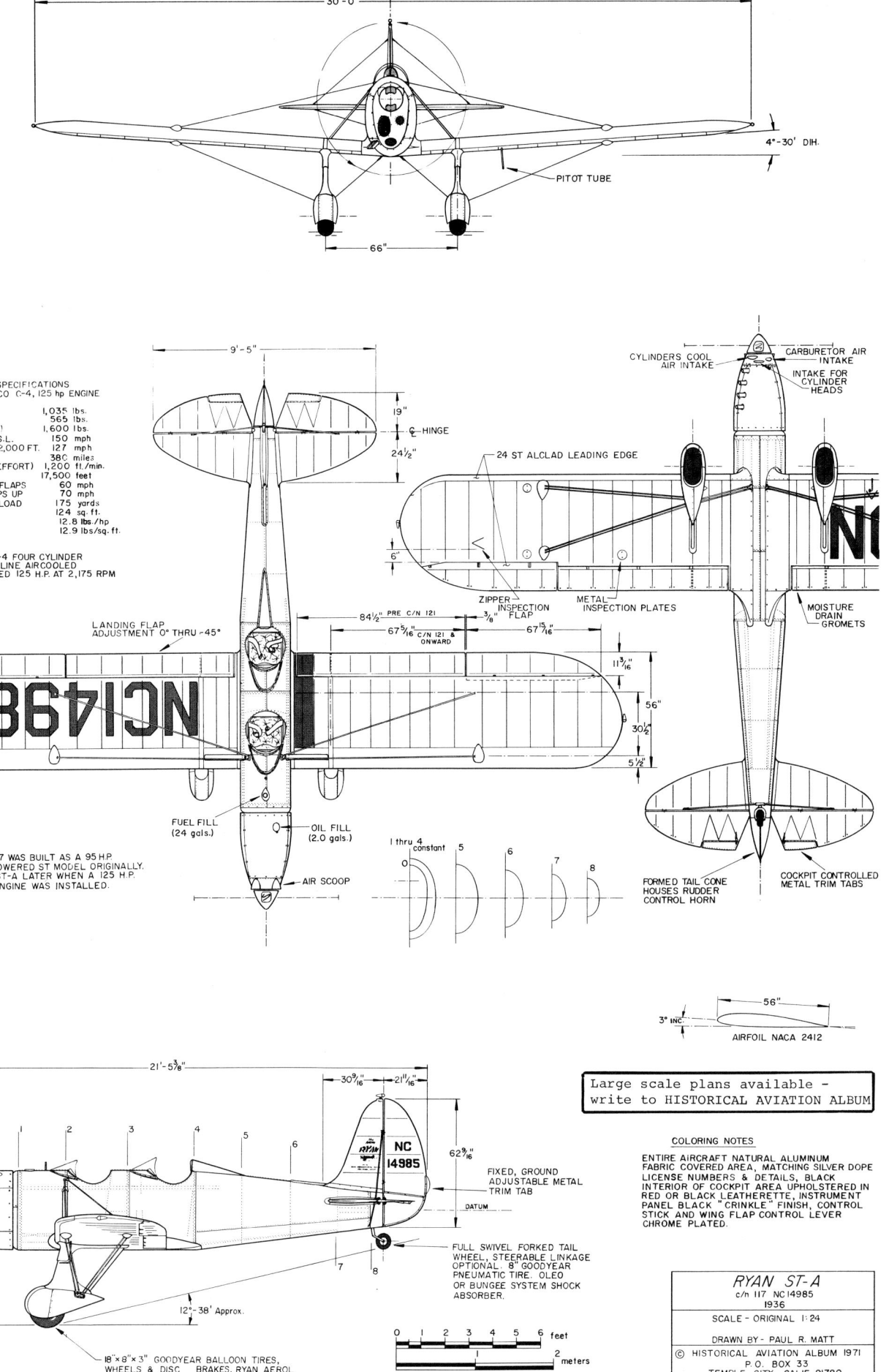

THE S-T

T. CLAUDE RYAN re-entered the aircraft manufacturing field with the "New Ryan" Sport Trainer in 1934. The S-T was designed over a period of nine months. The first sketches showed her with a straight turtle back and a quite angular fuselage. Ryan and two engineers, Millard Boyd and Will Vandermeer, refined the details to the well-known and classic beauty she is today.

With the help of A & P students, Ryan Aeronautical Co. built the prototype under the direction of Dan Burnett.

A number of engines were considered, among these were the 90 hp Gypsy, the 95 hp Menasco B 4 and the Menasco C 4 of 125 hp. The Cirrus engine used in the Great Lakes was also in the running as one of the first drawings showed this engine.

The prototype used c/n 101 and the last civilian aircraft built was c/n 355. A total of 316 "S-T series" airplanes were built. The last was c/n 514 for the Dutch. The two hundred serial range was not used for the ST, but rather the SC cabin planes. For complete details of this see the table of S-T series production.

The fuselage was made in two major parts, firewall and cockpit section and tail cone. These were both semi-monocoque construction. The cockpit area had four stringers running the full length, two under and inside the cockpit opening and two that supported the floor boards. The tail cone had three "stringers" formed by a 90° bend inward of one inch on each underlying skin. The skin of these planes is 24ST Alclad .032 thick and fabricated from flat sheets. With the exception of the engine, wheels, fairings, cowling, propeller and spinner, the entire aircraft was formed from flat sheets, streamlined tubing, round tubing of steel and aluminum.

When examining the pictures of the construction work on c/n 101, 102 and 103, note the wood patterns on the shop walls from which the shaping dies were made. These were developed from lead poured into plaster, and sand molds the shapes of which were reproductions of various sections of cowls, wheel pants, bulkheads, etc. The production dies were made of zinc and produced a very precise compound curve or flange.

Each wing was constructed with two solid spruce spars (not laminated) and 13 stamped aluminum alloy ribs, 8 steel compression ribs and five bays of drag and anti-drag wires. The airfoil section was NACA 2412 with the leading edge covered with .016 aluminum. Ailerons and flaps had steel tube spars which also served as a bearing. There were six on each wing and the female portion of these bearings were bronze blocks. In spite of relatively crude bearings, the ailerons were exceptionally light to the touch in flight. The flaps with their aluminum ribs and trailing edges were fabric covered and connected directly to the cockpit by a crank operated mechanism. This early type flap operation was from the rear cockpit only, and was replaced with a lever again only in the rear cockpit. The first major change to the airframe took place at this time. The flaps were shortened, and no longer extended into the stub wing area. No model or ATC change resulted from this modification. The first ship made with the short flaps was c/n 120, NC-16031. Production was easier, and the change had no effect on the flying qualities. The STM-2 aircraft, and the last civilian aircraft built had flap actuating levers in both cockpits.

All six tail surfaces were built with aluminum ribs, and trailing edges, but the spars and hinges were tubular steel.

Landing gear was the same type used on the Gee Bee

c/n 102   -G. S. Williams photo

c/n 128 flown by Tex Rankin. -Bill Yeager photo

racers, and consisted of a hinged treadle, and a Cleveland Air Oil shock strut. The tires, wheels and brakes were Goodyear.

The aircraft was basically a handmade plane. Each part was cut and formed by hand, then set up in jigs and welded or riveted by hand. This was a good system in the early and middle 1930's, but it spelled the end to this series of aircraft. With the coming of World War II, skilled labor was scarce and mass production methods were the only way.

All the civilian and some military ST aircraft were the STA-1 airframe. That is characterized for the following minor details of construction: heel brakes, no parking brake, fixed seats, and the longerons under the cockpit openings are inside of the fuselage. The STA-2 airframe had: toe brakes, parking brakes and seats adjustable by a handle to go up and forward and down and back. Longerons were lower on the outside of the fuselage to make the cockpits larger. There was no change in the ATC, and these models were built under both ATC 571 and 681.

In May, 1934 the company name had been changed to The Ryan Aeronautical Co.

The prototype "Sport Trainer" with its 95 hp Menasco was completed on the first of June, 1934. On June 8, John Fornasero made the first test flight from Lindbergh Field. The only problem seemed to be the propeller, and the ground adjustable metal prop was removed and a wood propeller was installed.

Number 101 was then flown to Mines Field in Los Angeles for final approval by the Department of Commerce. After just two weeks of test flights, she was issued ATC 541 on June 21, 1934. It really was not quite this simple or easy to receive the coveted ATC number. The fact is that destruction and static tests and constant supervision was carried on during every phase of the aircraft's construction. This static testing and construction work was recorded on both still and motion pictures. Fortunately, there are a number of copies of these series' pictures, including a 400 ft 16 mm film.

The ship was used by the students in flight instruction and many other purposes to promote and prove the new plane. The second and third ships were under construction when on December 19, 1934, a student pilot, Sanford Baldwin, was flying 101 over the Bay area. Captain John Towers of the U. S. Navy saw him doing aerobatics at a very low level. For no apparent reason except being too low or inexperienced, the pilot crashed the ship into the mud flats. There was no in flight structural or design failure, and the pilot was killed.

The second S-T 102 was personally delivered by Claude Ryan to Seattle, Washington. Unfortunately, NC-14909 was destined for a short life as she crashed April 7, 1937 at Pasco, Washington and was never rebuilt.

The S-T designation of this series of aircraft referred to serial numbers 101, 102, 104, 117 and 155 only. These planes were the only ships built with a 95 hp Menasco engine. None of these planes survive as such today.

103 was delivered to Peter Dana, a twenty-two year old student at the Ryan School who bought a package deal of a plane and flying lessons. He flew NC-14910 to a number of intracity records! San Diego to New York in 25 hours, 40 minutes and then beat his own record by doing it again in 22 hours, 6 min. He also established a "Tri-Flag" record by flying from Vancouver, B.C. to Tijuana, Mexico in 11 hours and 6 minutes.

NC-14952, c/n 108, with a C4 engine was the first Ryan STA shipped out of the continental U.S. She went to Honolulu in 1935 and was wrecked there.

John "Tex" Rankin flew NC-16039, c/n 128 to first place in the International Aerobatic Competition at St. Louis, Missouri on Memorial Day, 1937. The plane was a stock STA with a C 4 engine. The only modification made was to the propeller for more RPM. He and his partner "Put" Humphreys used this plane for exhibition of aerobatics for a number of years. Rankin lent his Ryan to Gladys O'Donnell for the Amelia Earhart Trophy Races of '36 and '37. In the 1936 handicap event, Gladys O'Donnell flew the forty miles at Los Angeles National Air Races in NC-16039 to a second place. The 1937 race at the Cleveland National Air Races she won the five lap 25 mile race in 11:34 minutes at 125.653 mph. This STA is still flying in California, and is now powered by a Menasco 134 hp D4-87 engine.

STA-Special c/n 141 started as a civilian model aircraft, and was sold new to Ted Brown, but ended up in the Nicaraguan National Guard, and was flown by Guard Officers for sport and training. I saw the plane in 1955 at the airport at Managua. She was immaculately maintained in flying condition. Some years later she was crossing Lake Managua and the engine quit. The story goes that her pilot could swim, but she could not. She was never recovered from her watery grave.

One of Tex Rankin's proteges was Harry Marshall, an advanced student at the Ryan School in 1938. He owned STA c/n 178, NC-16037, and had modified her so he could have smoke trails in his aerobatics. In a desert practice area known as Camp Kearney, he was putting on a low level

c/n 355, NC9 -Burton Kemp photo

"Grandaddy's Axe" c/n 198, NC18902

c/n 355, NC9E -Leo Kohn photo

c/n 188, NC18904 in Ohio, 1949

exhibition. The smoke system had not been tested properly, and caused enough back pressure in the Menasco's short modified stacks to stop it. He was inverted at low altitude at the time the engine stopped, and the plane stalled at 100 ft after rolling over. Marshall died shortly after the accident and the Ryan was not rebuilt.

The civil aviation cross-country cruise of the Aero Club of Brazil was won five years in a row by Anesio Amaral, Jr. in his Ryan STA c/n 127, and in 1939 Lt. James H. Gray flew an STA across the Andes from Santiago, Chile to Mendoza, Argentina at altitudes up to 17,000.

Number 355 was a special order sandwiched in among military orders, and was the last civilian machine built. She was delivered to the C.A.A. for use as a pilot check plane. Leonard Povey took delivery at the factory in 1939. Her registration number was NC-9 while she worked for the government, but this was changed to NC-9E after being sold. To this date, NC-9 (or N-9) has never been used again by the C.A.A. or the F.A.A. There are pictures of her with five different paint jobs, and even a closed canopy over both cockpits. I bought her in very disreputable condition in 1964, and flew her 900 miles home with only the oil pressure gauge working. Having never been the pilot of an STA before, it was a thrill and challenge.

In the late forties, a flying STA could be bought for about $900. In 1964, I paid $4200 for N-9E. By 1970, the price was up to $10,500, and in 1975 one sold for $18,000.

In the winter of 1965, I flew the completely redone NC9E to Florida and then to Nassau. The trip to Nassau from Fort Lauderdale is 200 miles over open ocean, quite a distance for a plane with only a surplus B-16 compass for navigation. In April, 1965 when returning from Harvard, Illinois, we hit a large bird right on the spinner. The result was instantaneous. The spinner came off and was hit by the propeller. This cracked the prop and broke two prop bolts. The spinner was hurled through the right wing, ripping off two feet of fabric. The propeller was now badly out of balance, but not enough to make me want to turn off the engine. All my thoughts were of the time Ed Bowman shut down the Menasco on c/n 157, NC-17353 because he lost the metal tip from one blade of his prop. This resulted in a badly bent Ryan because he needed a few more feet in the air to make an open field. In any case, we made it to Waukegan only to have the hangar roof fall on her that afternoon because of a tornado. NC-9E was repaired and flown to Virginia where she has remained stored for many years.

NC-14911 and NC-14910 were used by Tufts Edgcombe at Palwaukee, Illinois to train Naval officers to fly. When the program came to an end, NC-14910 was sold easily. As for her sister ship, she had a very bad reputation as a squirrelly and tempermental plane and nobody wanted her. She was rented occasionally by the hour, but few pilots flew her more than once. Her last moments of flight in 1944 with a solo student pilot at the controls, was a low approach for landing — so low she almost hit a hangar. At the last moment the pilot pulled up, but did not add power. NC-14911 stalled about fifty feet up and crashed: "Solving the problem of what to do with that cranky Ryan." The pilot was unharmed.

Women pilots were very successful and pleased with the Sport Trainer as the plane was light, responsive and easily controlled. Laura Ingalls purchased c/n 179 for aerobatics, and had it equipped at the factory with an inverted fuel system. She was a very famous pilot and it is too bad she did not choose to make any of her many records in this ship. The plane turned up being used by the Troy Flying Service, Troy, New York, and was involved in a very bad accident in 1944, in which both student and instructor were killed when the plane crashed in a forest.

The flashy little classic ST had not been ignored by Hollywood. "TOO HOT TO HANDLE", starring Myrna Loy, Walter Pidgeon and Clark Gable was made in 1938, with the "help" of a Ryan STA. Another film with the ST was "TEST PILOT", again with Myrna Loy, Clark Gable, and this time Spencer Tracy. "FIGHTER SQUADRON" used two ST's camouflaged and changed to look like retractable gear fighters. The painted wheel wells and British markings did not quite explain how the wheels would be retracted when the wing wires are braced against them. Another "British Fighter" was an STA in disguise in Fred MacMurray's and Errol Flynn's "DIVE BOMBER". In the picture section, we have a print of NC-17300, the plane used in the "HOWIE WING" movie serial.

After the second World War, the Sport-Trainers fell into a period during which they were unwanted and neglected. This resulted in aircraft which were poorly maintained and had many problems. A good flying STA could be bought for very little, and damaged ships were junked, as they were not worth repairing.

A boy in Connecticut bought c/n 198, NC-18902 in this period and planned to fly her around the country. He got as far as Fort Lauderdale, and took off East over the ocean when the engine quit. She did not make it gliding back to shore, and crashed in shallow water causing very little damage. She was shipped back to Connecticut and sold to a dealer in Rhode Island. He stored the fuselage in a barn, and the wings and tail in a chicken coop. Years went by, and he needed the space so the fuselage went "out back in the woods". Some boys painted a target on her side and shot her full of holes and ground squirrels made nests in the gas tank when the bottom fell out. In 1966, an airline Captain told me of some ailerons and flaps he had seen for an ST. A phone call in February revealed that the flaps and ailerons were for sale. But what of the rest of the plane? She was under a foot of snow and the owner had not looked her over for years. Two months went by and another call. The report was very negative, but I took a chance and drove from Chicago to Rhode Island and bought the "parts". The next problem was to identify the plane and get the papers. Parts were carefully cleaned, and the fuselage bore c/n 198, and the left wing was from c/n 179. The FAA records showed c/n 198 still registered to Arthur McEwen. A phone call resulted in contacting the "boy", now a Lt. Colonel in the Air Force home on leave for the funeral of his father. It was the first time he had been at that address for more than a short visit in twenty years. He had all the papers and log books and agreed to send them to me. Six months later, c/n 198 rolled out for her first flight in twenty years on June 10, 1967.

This plane is the classic case of "Granddaddy's Axe". Even though it has had five new handles and two new heads, it is still Granddaddy's axe. The cowl and all the fairings were made in Colorado by a man remembered only as Joe. The Menasco engine was surplus government stock from Canada. The tail came from the garage of a mechanic who worked at Palwaukee in 1944, and was reported to be from c/n 104. The left stub wing and gas tank came from an unknown Ryan in Connecticut. This Ryan after being rebuilt was the most stable aircraft I ever flew, and also the slowest STA on record. She had no bad habits, could be trimmed at any speed for hands off flying and cruised at 95 mph. She still flies in Michigan.

One of the most important factors in keeping the early ST aircraft flying resulted from a decision by the Royal Canadian Air Force in 1941. The R.C.A.F. used DeHavilland Gipsy 145 hp engines in many of their primary trainers. Because the supply of parts and engines was threatened by the European war, they bought "backup" Menasco engines. The total order was for 200 engines; those delivered were mostly D4-87's, but some were D 4's. All were tested, pickled and stored throughout the war. In 1946, they were sold on the surplus market, and ever since a few each year have come home to power America's Ryans.

Every once in a while we come across a picture showing a old STA in an interesting situation. One such photo was taken on a rainy day, 1949 in Ohio. It showed NC-18904, c/n 188 being towed out of a harvested cornfield by a team of horses. It is too bad interesting stories and incidents such as these are not recorded so we may know more of the facts.

Bill Dodd's Guatemalan STM, N-11D was seen perhaps more than any other during the early 1960's. He put on exhibitions of aerobatics at air shows and fly-ins. His was always the best act as the little orange and silver Ryan rolled and looped through a flawless sequence at very low altitude. Bill knows the Ryan, and her capabilities better than any pilot and only showed the maneuvers she does the best. This made it possible for him to win the Amateur Aerobatic Championship at Ottumwa, Iowa, three years running, 1961-62-63.

This Ryan was equipped with an inverted fuel system, but had no other changes. My first flight in an STM was in his ship, and maybe I should have expected something when he strapped me in using two seat belts and a shoulder harness. At no more than two hundred feet, he rolled, inverted and left the pattern. An hour after landing, I sold my PT-22 and three weeks later I owned my first STA, N-9E. The only "fault" with Bill and his Ryan is that they make aerobatics look so easy. This is very disappointing to the rest of us trying the same maneuvers, and slopping and mushing through them. The registration of his plane recently was changed to N-302D — the plane was just recovered and is in flying condition.

Dario Toffenetti is the owner of NC-17631, c/n 166. Dario found the Ryan in 1965 in the basement of a Chicago apartment house. She was complete and undamaged, mainly needing paint and covering. The work was completed in 1967, and she has been flown every year since. The plane has won several awards including the T. Claude Ryan Trophy for the "Most Original Ryan ST" at Ottumwa.

NC-17345, c/n 148 was totally restored to beautiful flying condition, and then sold twice very quickly. The new owner had recently recovered from a heart attack. He started the long ferry flight from Florida to Ohio. He made two stops for fuel and was nearing an airport in Georgia for a third landing. There were no witnesses to c/n 148's last moments of flight, but she was found badly bent in the woods with a dead pilot at the controls. The autopsy showed the elderly pilot had died from a heart attack prior to impact. The Ryan had flown herself in the tops of the trees, and then fallen almost straight down after slowing up. The wreck went to California, and was partly rebuilt by John Gokchoff and then sold and shipped to Virginia where her present owner will have her flying again by middle 1975.

NC-17364, c/n 177 led a hard life. Her logs show 3850 hours, three hard ground loops, and three times on her back. This is the highest known time of any "ST" series aircraft. Over a period of 10 years her owner had restored the ship except for painting. He was transferred from Kansas to Ohio, and started the ferry flight in July, 1972. The weather was good and the visibility excellent until he reached Missouri. Many fires, presumably from the manufacture of charcoal, caused a low laying cloud of smoke over the hill country near Williamsby, Missouri. The pilot with 10 hours in type, let down to go under the smoke haze, as he had no radio navigation equipment. The propeller hub bolts failed at just this time. Unfortunately, the "open" field picked for the emergency landing had an unseen fence across it. The Ryan touched down and rolled about 10 feet hitting the fence which literally tore her to pieces. The wreckage was sold and rebuilt.

The reason we have shown the last registered owner, and disposition of Ryans not currently flying, is to try to get some of these back in the air. Any information can become a starting point for finding a Ryan damaged after accidents or just stored. Most of course, are gone. But in the last 15 years, four have been found in barns, five returned to this country from the Pacific, seven came back from Guatemala, two from Mexico (one STM and one SCW) and one found in an apartment house. There are rumors of two float planes in Venezuela, and I hope this list will be added to.

At the West Coast Ryan Fly-In 1972, T. Claude Ryan flew in from San Luis Obispo to Paso Robles in the rear seat of Jim Dewey's STM and won the plaque for the "oldest Ryan" at the fly-in. He and William Wagner showed films of the building, testing and flying of the 'Spirit of St. Louis' and the original ST.

—Dorr B. Carpenter

THE EXPORT STM

The STM (Sport Trainer Military) aircraft were built in accordance with the type certificate of their civilian counterparts. Basically the military models had crank starters (direct drive, hand crank Bendix starter — not inertia) and the insignia of the country to which it belonged. STM planes delivered to Central and South America were usually flown to their destination with the front cockpit covered, the front windshield removed and the machine guns, if any, not installed.

MEXICO

The first order for trainers was made by Mexico; six unarmed STM aircraft with Menasco supercharged C4-S engines. They were delivered by rail, and then little was heard of them for many years. They were reportedly used at Monterrey and Mexico City, and then they were not heard from for a long time.

However, a Mexican "ST" did come back to America. She is c/n 184, formerly No. 3 of the Mexican Air Force. This plane was never registered in Mexico, and had been in storage since the war, except for a period she was registered as N7828C. She is now registered and flying as NC17360, first in California, then in Texas, and now in Illinois.

HONDURAS

The second foreign order was from Honduras for armed STM aircraft in May, 1938. These were single seater fighter trainers with a single fixed machine gun mounted on the fuselage. The guns themselves were installed by the Honduran Air Force. All three were delivered by air in an overflight of Mexico under the command of Capt. Malcolm Stewart H.A.F., and two Ryan factory employees, William Sloan and Harry Cameron. They left San Diego June 13, 1938 for Tegucigalpa, Honduras. An American Air Force Colonel tried to trace them in 1974 and found only a Menasco engine.

GUATEMALA

The Guatemalans placed two orders for STM aircraft in July and December, 1938. The first order was for unarmed trainers, and the second was for armed planes, and equipment to arm the preceding order. Two 7mm Colt machine guns were mounted on the wings firing outboard of the

propeller arc. The only change in the structure of the wing was an extra rib to support the gun and ammunition. Bill Dodd's Guatemalan (c/n 302) Ryan still carries this extra rib. Seven of these Ryans survive. They were brought back to St. Petersburg, Fla. in 1958 by Dick Spencer. He was flying a loaded Curtiss C-46 to Guatemala and would have returned empty but for the Ryans. Nine engines and enough parts to make seven aircraft and some extra tail cones and pieces were delivered to Hower Aircraft in Florida. Spencer's idea was to trade the whole lot for one flying Ryan. The result is that c/n 192, 193, 195, 197, 302, 303 and 304 came home.

BOLIVIA

Arrangement was made to give Bolivia Ryans under the Lend-Lease program. Only one was delivered, in 1940, and she was a civilian STA-Special NC18905, c/n 199. The delivery flight was made to Cochabama airfield without any trouble. But the aircraft was severely damaged on her first flight from Cochabama, probably because of the 7000 ft. altitude of the air field, and the very heavy General who occupied the front cockpit. Years later she was reported derelict and forgotten in the Pan American Grace Hangar at Cochabama. One effort has been made to locate her, but without success.

CHINA

A group of STM-2 aircraft were ordered by the Republic of China in November, 1939. The contracts were negotiated through China Airmotive Company, a purchasing agent for the Far East. This agreement also granted manufacturing rights for the ST aircraft to the Central Aircraft Manufacturing Company at Loiwing, China. The manufacturing rights were never used. The order called for 50 land plane trainers, 48 of them two-seater unarmed planes and 2 one place armed fighter trainers. They were all equipped with C 4S-2 engines, and two had a single machine gun mounted inside the fuselage and firing through the propeller. All planes were shipped from San Diego unmarked and crated, the first leaving in February, 1940. They arrived at Loiwing by a round about route. For the last part of the trip over the mountains, some flew in and others were trucked in. The last planes arrived in the spring of 1941, and were painted with the markings of Nationalist China and then dispatched to Poasham, Kunming, Chengtu and Ipin.

The Central Aircraft Factory at Loiwing was bombed by the Japanese and six Ryan STM aircraft were destroyed. There were twenty Ryans at Kunming late in 1941, and about half were damaged or destroyed in bombing attacks. Kunming in Hunan Province was a major Flying Tiger base (AVG). We have a report from the assistant maintenance chief, George J. Brice of the 2nd Pursuit, pertaining to the Ryans on the field from January, 1942 to December, 1942. He states that during the year, the 2nd Pursuit was at Kunming, and the Ryans were not used by the Chinese.

About twelve planes were parked at the field in revetments. The ground maintenance people were not allowed to fly the P-40 aircraft, so they looked longingly at the little Ryans. One day, using mostly bluff and no authority, a group of them simply went over and took a Ryan and towed it to their area. Although the Ryans were guarded by Chinese soldiers, the Americans were not challenged. The Ryan was checked over, found to have faulty magnetos, which were repaired. For about a month the Chinese allowed their plane to be used for the sport of the A.V.G. The day came when a squad of soldiers came and took the Ryan back. At this point most people would have left well enough alone, but not this bunch. They repeated the original take over about once a month for the remainder of the year.

— Dorr B. Carpenter

RYANS IN THE FAR EAST

A SHORT, colorful page of aviation history was written in the skies of the Far East by the little Ryan STM trainers in early World War II.

Operated in Java, by the Netherlands East Indies Air Arm, called "Wapen der Militaire Luchtvaart van het Koninklijk Nederlands Indische Leger" or ML for short were 60 Ryan STM-2 trainers. This was the army operation from a base at Bandoeng. All 60 of these planes were either destroyed by Japanese action or captured intact. These were airplanes c/n 407-446 (RO-10 to RO-49) and 495-514 (RO-50 to RO-69).

There were 48 STM-S2 operated by the Dutch Naval Air Service, called "Marine Luchtvaart Dienst" or MLD. These were operated both as landplanes with wheels or seaplanes with floats. These were c/n 447-494 (S-11 to S-58).

It is largely the story of these MLD or Navy airplanes that is known for while 15 were lost during the war, either from training accidents or Japanese action, 34 were evacuated to Australia. But, before they were evacuated they wrote a courageous aviation story in the skies of Java.

Ryan shipped the first 12 MLD airplanes on November 18, 1940 aboard the SS Hoegh Silver Dawn. Eight more left on the MS Java on December 7, four more on the MS Klipfontein on December 21. Eight more were delivered by the factory in December, 16 more in January 1941. Before the outbreak of war on December 8, 1941 (the 8th in the Far East, the 7th in the USA) eight planes had been lost. Two by fatal accidents on August 2 and 10 and S-43 (c/n 479) by fire in October. Reports indicate that the STM-S2 on floats was difficult to recover from a flat spin.

From December 8 to February 16, 1942, seven more planes were lost, two by Japanese attack on February 3. On the 17th of February, the remaining 34 airplanes were shipped aboard the MS Tjinegara to Australia where they were operated for a short time by the MLD. When Dutch flying training was transferred to Jackson, Mississippi these planes were transferred to the RAAF. No. 2 and 3 communication units of the RAAF used these planes and fuselage codes JU and DB were painted on the planes.

Back in Java . . .

Twelve American and twelve Dutch instructors were training pilots at Moro N.B. "Little Pensacola". The seaplane base was on Soerabaja Bay adjoining the land plane base.

The first class were partly trained Dutch pilots who escaped the Nazis, and the later classes were composed of Dutch colonials from Java, Sumatra, Borneo and half cast Chinese and native Javanese. When the war began, the students were far enough along to fly the Ryan land planes inland about 50 miles of Malang. Some of the pilots in this operation had as little as three hours solo time and it must have been quite an adventure. These planes were ferried approximately 200 miles to Bandoeng at the west end of Java. A number of students ran out of gas because of poor navigation and made forced landings in sawahs (rice paddies) but the ships held up so well that in spite of several turnovers none of the pilots were injured.

Very few Ryans were lost in training, and those were with only solo students at the controls. The unarmed seaplanes were sometimes surprised aloft by Japanese aircraft, and had to rely on maneuverability to escape. It was not easy and the Ryans often returned to their base with bullet holes and parts shot away.

U. S. Navy Lt. Earl Lee was one of the American instructors in Java. His brother, oddly enough, worked at the Ryan Factory. He liked the STM, particularly those on floats, as every landing was a new experience. With a student in the rear cockpit, Lt. Lee was making touch and go landings on Soerabaja Bay. Just as the plane settled in the water, a geyser shot up directly in the ship's path. Lee took control instantly, and gave the Ryan full power. They had been attacked by a Japanese Val. The Ryan was flying just above the water when she was hit. This time she went down for good and sank, but instructor and student swam ashore.

A short time later, Lt. Lee and another student were caught at 7000 ft by a Japanese Zero fighter. The first pass by the Zero completely missed as the Japanese pilot miscalculated the Ryan's speed. With the Menasco at full power, they played cat and mouse in and out of the clouds, driving and spiraling toward the bay. Finally, just above the water, the Zero made a good pass and hit the Ryan repeatedly, killing the student. A second Zero joined forces, but after two more passes gave up the chase. This action had taken 25 minutes, and the Ryan was still airborne. Lee surmised that his floats would not hold him, so he elected to land on a flooded rice paddy.

Few Ryans were actually shot out of the sky by enemy action, but many never flew again after landing. The STM-S2 seaplanes were usually flown inland and landed on flooded rice paddies during air raids and hidden until all was clear and then returned to resume pilot training. The Ryan could easily out-maneuver one fighter because of the beautiful handling qualities and control response of the Ryan even when dragging along a pair of floats.

One use the seaplanes were put to was flying supplies to ships hidden in coastal harbours and outposts along the island coastline. On long coast patrols cans of gas were carried in the front cockpit, and the plane was landed in sheltered harbors to refuel. A few STM-2S aircraft were sent to Borneo early in the war for patrol duty.

A Javanese pilot who lost his wife in a bombing attack, took up a seaplane trainer and deliberately engaged a Japanese Zero. He was able to crash his Ryan into the Zero; both pilots were killed. At the time of this action, February, 1942, the Japanese had invaded the Malayan Peninsula, and were attacking Java with flights of up to 100 aircraft. The Dutch had crated 34 Ryans and loaded them aboard a ship in the harbor for evacuation to Australia. It is a good thought that maybe the Japanese bombs missed that important ship because of the actions of this brave pilot and his little Ryan.

At least five Ryans served the Japanese Imperial Air Force with the rising sun painted on their wings and fuselages.

Lt. H. F. C. Holts, a Royal Netherlands pilot captured on Java, escaped and reported that he saw Japanese pilots flying the Ryans, doing aerobatics and formation flying. The indication is that they were used for sport, and two of the Ryans were seen to have a midair collision.

c/n 441 as S-11 (see cover)-Ryan(Wagner)

STM-2 c/n 426 in Netherlands Army markings

c/n 409 (RO12) and 410 (RO13) NEI Army

c/n 454 and 450 (S-14) operational

NEI Navy line up of 18 STM-2 on Java

Only way to prop a floatplane! STM-S2

c/n 487 as STM-2 in Java

c/n 457 N8146 restored as original S-21

THE SAGA OF STM-S2 c/n 476

1 STM-S2 c/n 476 starts its journey in December 1940, leaving San Diego and the Ryan factory for shipment to the Netherlands East Indies (Java). Arrived February 1941 and used by the Dutch Marine Air Arm (MLD) out of Soerabaja as STM-S2 No. S-40.

2 By February 17, 1942, only 34 of the original 108 STM airplanes are left. These are shipped to the Royal Australian Air Force. No. 476 is one of these planes. It was delivered to the RAAF August 21, 1942 at Mascot Aerodrome and flew as A50-30.

3 On June 12, 1946, the 26 surviving STM airplanes are sold surplus to Brown & Dureau of Melbourne. No. 476 has accumulated 170 hours of military flying and is overhauled at this time. Registered as VH-AGZ, No. 476 flies from Moorabbin (Melbourne) and makes two trips to Tasmania (over 200 miles water!) and back. Also flies to Berwick, Kerang and Yarrawonga. On August 3, 1957 she hit high tension lines at Corowa and wrecked. Total time is 402 hours.

3 First flight test after repairs, on December 25, 1959. New tail cone (from c/n 448, Dutch Navy S-12) is fitted and front cockpit reskinned. Owned by Mr. B. Buchanan, Seymour, flights include Warranambool, Benhalla, Ballarat and Broadford. Sold in 1964 to Mr. E. R. D. Mackay with 555 hours.

5 January 1969, Dorr Carpenter goes to Australia and buys No. 476 with 597 hours total time. Dorr flies it from Jerico to Sydney via Roma, Cliffton and Scone. January 20, 1969, Rex Aviation (Bankstown) crates No. 476 for shipment to the USA.

6 Shipped via the Australian Gem steamship from Sydney to New York City, No. 476 returns home after 29 years in the Far East. From New York to Lake Bluff is via truck. Dorr Carpenter checks her over and relicensed No. 476 as N288Y with 613 hours time.

4 Flying the 1300 mile trip from Melbourne to Rosedale, the engine quits and No. 476 groundloops on landing at Charleyville. A new left landing gear is fitted and on March 5, 1964 it arrives at Rosedale (Jerico Station)
Flights include trips to Kensington, Long Reach, Blackall and Barcaldine.

7 Dorr flies No. 476 between July and October 1969. At that time it is sold to Jeff Cannon and shipped to him in California via United Airlines DC-8 freighter. It is shortly sold to Mike Cuddy of Thousand Oaks who takes it out of service with 630 hours total time for a major overhaul in December 1971.

8 STM-S2 No. 476 remained stored from December 1971 through January 1975. During this time the wings and flying surfaces are recovered. Purchased by Mitch Mayborn in January 1975 and hauled from California to Dallas, Texas via truck. Restoration to flying status should be complete by fall 1975 and as N7779, No. 476 should be flying once more.

After shipment to Australia, the Ryans and some floats remained on the Sydney docks for a long period, and because they were in their original crates, gave rise to the rumor, that they were new from America.

The reported price paid for the 35 planes and spares was £15,000. They were used for refresher training and transport missions with Nos. 1, 2 and 3 communications' units of the Royal Austrailian Air Force. It was neither war, nor time, which was to destroy a large number of Ryans at one stroke, but a violent storm in April, 1945. They were in a hangar at Evans Head, with wings off because of an order by the Air Board, "to conserve aviation fuel". The end result was the destruction of five planes, as they were destroyed by the storm.

At war's end, the surviving 26 aircraft were sold by the Commonwealth Disposals Commission for an average of £400 each with engine, and £200 each without engine. They were purchased by Brown and Dureau, Ltd. of Melbourne.

At least three STMs were fitted with deHavilland "Gipsy Major" engines by Dave Bourke, chief engineer for Geelong Airways. He is also responsible for the conversion of Elmer L. Pickles, 1937 STA c/n 132, to a Gipsy engine. Elmer's Ryan was undergoing a slow repair after being damaged many years ago, but should be flying by 1975.

Dave is the owner of c/n 471, VH-BWQ on which he has been working intermittently for many years. It should be nearly perfect, as she has a new engine, and only 200 hours on the airframe. He is considered by most to be the most knowledgeable man on the subject of Ryan's in his country. He also designed the two major modifications used on these planes: the strengthening of the center-section landing gear wire attachments, and the stringers between No. 2 and 3 bulkheads, both now required by the DCA. His interest in supplying information, manuals, and parts is very instrumental in keeping the Ryans flying.

Ryan identification plates are located in the back of the rear cockpit on the right side. The plate is the same "New Ryan" type used on the earlier models, and they were built in accordance with all specifications for ATC 681 (STA Special) and marked STM-S2.

Three Ryans were used in Hong Kong after being first registered but not flown, in Australia. One of these, c/n 452 was registered there as VR-HDL. All three were used for student instruction for a number of years. Number 452 was shipped to Norway, and registered as LN-TVF. It was brought to the United States in 1967 by Capt. J. Bassett of the USAF, and remained stored in New York. In the winter of 1969 as N9761 was flown west as far as Frankfort, Illinois where she stayed awaiting magneto repairs and warmer weather. Then she continued on to Washington state, having completed a round the world trip in thirty years. The second plane, VH-AGX, VR-HDM remained in Hong Kong and lay derelict behind a hangar until the early 1970's, and then was sold and shipped east to an American owner in Tacoma, Washington. At this time (1975) she is not registered or in flying condition. The third Hong Kong Ryan number 494 left China for the Philippine Islands, and was converted to a modern flat Lycoming 0-435 engine. PI-C324 (PI-471) was her fourth civilian registration in three countries after flying for two nations in war time. Number 494 is now in the U.S., and flying under an old ST registration number N14911.

Jeriderie in New South Wales is the home of the two well cared for Ryans. One VH-AHC is fitted with a long range fuel tank in the front cockpit in place of the seat. The other, VH-AHD, is standard configuration. Both ships are polished aluminum and silver, and have been owned by the same man for over twenty years.

— Dorr B. Carpenter

Australian STM's were all "A50" series

Ex-NEI STM in Australian marks   -RAAF

STM-2 c/n 463 as RAAF A50-12   -RAAF

RAAF put STM in service July, 1942

c/n 457 as VH-BXN ex A50-30 and S-21

c/n 482 as VH-CXR ex A50-19 and S-46

c/n 459 as VH-AGD ex A50-11 and S-23

STA Special c/n 339   -Pete Bulban photo

c/n 475 as VH-AGR ex A50-9 and S-39

c/n 492 as VH-AHC ex A50-29 and S-56

STA c/n 174, NC17396 about 1950

STK c/n 406 with three-piece windows

ST Series Production

c/n	Date 1st Delivery	Initial Registration	Model	Engine/hp.	First Owner	Most recent owner/date license/remarks
101	6-8-34	NX14223	S-T	B4/95	Ryan Aeronautical	Became NC14223. Crashed San Diego 12-19-34.
102	4-6-35	NC14909	S-T	B4/95	L. Peterson	E. Weller, Crashed Pasco, Wa. 4-7-37
103	5-21-35	NC14910	STA	C4/125	Peter Dana	Lynch & Caravetta (NY) 10-19-55. (?)
104	5-16-35	NC14911	S-T	B4/95	H. P. Bingham	T. Edgecombe. Crash 1944. C/n 104 now on c/n 494
105	7-20-35	NC14912	STA	C4/125	W. M. Miller	J & F. Medlin (ID) 1946 Civil A/C Register
106	7-1-35	NC14913	STA	C4/125	J. VonEyssenhardt	Air Activities, Inc (Texas) 4-12-48
107	7-16-35	NC14914	STA	C4/125	Tex Rankin	Air Service, Inc (Ga) 7-15-37, Crashed Atlanta
108	7-30-35	NC14952	STA	C4/125	James Dodd	Same, crashed Honolulu Hawaii
109	11-6-35	NC14953	STB	C4/125	Cliff Durant	W. Brown (Ca) 4-15-39, Crash 6-5-39 Sacramento
110	9-21-35	NC14954	STA	C4/125	Capt. G. Hancock	Dr. E. Cramer (Ca) 1965. Rebuilding in 1975
111	1-23-36	NC14955	STA	C4/125	Irwin (dealer)	H. Barnes (NC) 11-13-40. Burned 5-5-41
112	1-13-36	NC14956	STA	C4/125	Ted Brown	Wrecked at Palm Springs, Ca. 8-3-37
113	1-21-36	NC14957	STA	C4/125	Irwin (dealer)	Fred Barber (GA), 8-25-70, rebuilding 1975
114	1-20-36	NC14982	STA	C4/125	W. Dillingham	Mark Hoskins (WA) Stored damaged cond. 1975
115	1-23-36	NC14983	STA	C4/125	Irwin (dealer)	T. Berry (KS), being rebuilt 1975
116	1-23-36	NC14984	STA	C4/125	F. Farrel (Irwin)	c/n 116 flying on PT-20 airframe c/n ?
117	1-23-36	NC14985	S-T	B4/95	Irwin (dealer)	New England Aero Inst. (NH) Flying condition
118	6-7-36	NC14986	STA	C4/125	J. Schoellkopf	Capt. Simick (MI) Flying 1975 as N1151
119	5-22-36	NC14987	STA	C4/125	Dr. L. Boldridge	Baldridge, crash 11-21-37 Charlotte, NC
120	7-17-36	NC16031	STA	C4/125	Maj. Hugh Watson	Ryan Aeronautical (CA) per 1946 C.A.R.
121	5-30-36	NC16032	STA-Spl.	C4-S/150	J. W. Thorne	R. P. Matthews (AZ) 4-26-48 (?)
122	7-17-36	NC16033	STA	C4/125	Irwin (dealer)	Robertson A/C (MO) 4-16-42, cancelled 4-21-48
123	7-17-36	NC16034	STA	C4/125	Irwin (dealer)	J. D. Finger (NY) airworthiness expired 9-40
124	7-17-36	NC16035	STA	C4/125	Irwin (dealer)	John Janicki (NY) scrapped 10-15-48
125	7-17-36	NC16036	STA	C4/125	Irwin (dealer)	Memphis Flying Club (TN) 8-20-53 (?)
126	8-13-36	PP-TBM	STA	C4/125	A. L. Seabra	To Brazil, F. M. Filho. Certificate exp. May '45
127	9-10-36	PP-TBQ	STA	C4/125	A. Amaral, Jr.	To Sao Paulo, Brazil. U.S. NC16038 cancelled
128	9-12-36	NC16039	STA	C4/125	Tex Rankin	Harold Sparks (CA). Flying 1975
129	9-18-36	NC16040	STA	C4/125	J. D. McKean	Morton Air Service (NV). Crashed 4-15-43
130	10-7-36	NC16041	STA	C4/125	Betty Lund	A/C Industries Co. Burned in hangar 6-19-44
131	11-6-36	NC16042	STA	C4/125	Joe Lewis	Crashed Corning, CA 10-9-38
132	10-22-36	VH-UZQ	STA	C4/125	Ken Frewin	E. Pickles. Flying, Australia, VH-BWQ.
133	11-11-36	NC16044	STA	C4/125	R. Archbold	W. F. Taylor (PA), crashed 10-3-44
134	11-14-36	NC17300	STA	C4/125	R. Archbold	Wood Flying Service (TN) 1946 C.A.R.
135	11-25-36	NC17301	STA	C4/125	John Lyon	Earle Hansen (ID). Burned up 4-3-41
136	12-5-36	NC17302	STA	C4/125	A. C. Goddard	Amarillo Air Serv. Accident 5-15-41
137	12-7-36	NC17303	STA	C4/125	Whitney (dealer)	R. Zenock (NJ). Accident 9-24-52
138	12-31-36	NC17304	STA	C4/125	Ted Brown (dealer)	Accident, Inglewood, CA 8-27-37
139	1-7-37	NC17305	STA	C4/125	Whitney (dealer)	D. F. Gutridge (CA), 6-3-48 (?)
140	1-21-37	NC17306	STA	C4/125	Franklin Rose	Webbs Flying Service (ID) Accident 5-29-41
141	2-4-37	NC17307	STA-Spl.	C4S/150	Ted Brown (dealer)	Nicaraguan Nat'l Guard. Crash Lake Managua 1938

STA c/n 156 with Lycoming O-360 (before)

STA c/n 156 back to Menasco   -Edwin Power

The STW c/n 338 with Warner engine -Ryan

Tex Rankin with STA c/n 128 -Underwood

STA c/n 118, N14986   -David Menard

STA c/n 105 with early cowling   -B. Kemp

STA Special c/n 188 NC18904   -Leo Kohn

STA c/n 118, N1151 (Ex-N14986) -Carpenter

ST Series Production

142	2-24-37	(?)	STA	C4/125	Haller Aviation	Shipped to South Africa, history unknown
143	3-6-37	NC17343	STA	C4/125	DeMorr Aviation	Troy Flyers, Inc (NY), accident 11-13-43
144	3-10-37	NC17344	STA	C4/125	Howard Batt	J & F Medlin (ID) 1946 C.A.R.
145	3-19-37	(?)	STA	C4/125	Haller Aviation	Shipped to South Africa, history unknown
146	3-19-37	(?)	STA	C4/125	Haller Aviation	Shipped to South Africa, history unknown
147	3-24-37	VH-UYN	STA	C4/125	Aeroflite (Sidney)	J. Meehan, Australia. Crash 1-9-48
148	3-24-37	NC17345	STA	C4/125	Central Aircraft	John Crouse (VA). Flying 1975
149	4-13-37	NC17346	STA	C4/125	John Roulstone	Dave Conoley (TX). Flying 1975
150	4-22-37	NC17347	STA	C4/125	Whitney (dealer)	Embry-Riddle Co. (FL). Crash 8-7-46
151	4-22-37	NC17348	STA	C4/125	Whitney (dealer)	J Gosney (CO) Flying '75 w/Ranger. N42X to N27JG
152	4-10-37	NC17349	STA	C4/125	Roberta Lupton	J. McCreary. Wreck 11-9-44.(See c/n 195)
153	4-22-37	NC17350	STA	C4/125	Whitney (dealer)	J. James (MO) per 1946 C.A.R.
154	4-22-37	NC17351	STA	C4/125	Whitney (dealer)	John Kane (TX). Flying 1975 as N633X
155	4-22-37	(?)	S-T	B4/95	Haller Aviation	Shipped to South Africa, history unknown
156	4-22-37	NC17352	STA-Spl.	C4S/150	Whitney (dealer)	Edwin Power (CA). Flying 1975
157	5-1-37	NC17353	STA	C4/125	Ryan School	E. J. Bowman, Denver, CO. 1964. Stored damaged
158	5-17-37	ZS-AKZ	STA	C4/125	S. African Flyng	Shipped to South Africa, history unknown.
159	5-11-37	NC17354	STA	C4/125	Brayton Flyng Svc.	A. McKinnis (MN). Crash Minneapolis 4-8-40
160	6-24-37	NC17355	STA	C4/125	Bill Joy	Ryan School of Aero. (CA) 1946 C.A.R.
161	6-11-37	NC17356	STA	C4/125	Ben Hazleton	Canton Aviation Co. (OH) Crash 4-28-48
162	7-7-37	NC17357	STA	C4/125	Booth-Henning	W. Grottkau (CA) 1946 C.A.R.
163	7-16-37	NC17358	STA	C4/125	Bill Joy (dealer)	R. P. Joy, Jr (MI) Accident 8-6-37
164	7-25-37	NC17359	STA-Spl.	C4S/150	Ryan School	A. R. Cuellar (TX) Accident 1957 written off
165	8-19-37	YV-G-TR3	STA	C4/125	G. Tamayo	Shipped to Venezuela, history unknown
166	8-7-37	NC17361	STA	C4/125	Booth-Henning	Dorr B. Carpenter. Rebuilding 1976
167	9-7-37	NC17362	STA	C4/125	C. B. Rians	J & F Medlin (ID) Accident 10-8-47
168	8-17-37	NC17363	STA	C4/125	Haller Aviation	Shipped to South Africa, history unknown
169	8-17-37	(?)	STA	C4/125	Haller Aviation	Shipped to South Africa, history unknown
170	9-1-37	NC17365	STA	C4/125	Wm. Stewart	L. I. Aretz (IN) Destroyed 10-18-40
171	8-27-37	NC17366	STA	C4/125	Bill Joy (dealer)	General Aeronautic Corp (MI) Crash 9-23-40
172	9-15-37	NC17367	STA	C4/125	John Morrell	George Tork (NY) FAA listed thru 1970
173	8-30-37	NC17368	STA-Spl.	C4S/150	Spence	Crash N.Y. C/n (P. Dacy) assigned STM (?)
174	7-26-37	NC17369	STA-Spl.	C4S/150	R. Card	A. V. Tidmore (PA) Flying 1975
175	(?)	NC17370	STA	C4/150	Ryan School	G. H. Montgomery (TN) Accident 6-9-44
176	(?)	NC17371	STA	C4/125	Ryan School	J & F Medlin (ID) Destroyed by fire 2-8-45
177	1-4-38	NC17364	STA	C4/125	W. D. Bassett	Dorr Carpenter (IL) Flying 1975
178	12-6-37	NC16037	STA	C4/125	Harry Marshall	G. Hadsell (CA). 7-11-41 (?)
179	5-7-38	NC18901	STA	C4/125	Laura Ingalls	Troy Flyers Inc (NY) Crashed 1944
180	8-2-38	NACA-96	STA-Spl.	C4S/150	NACA	J. Billhymer (MD) Registered N180Y (?)
181	10-5-37	NC18903	STA-Spl.	C4S/150	Mary Pike	To PP-THJ (Brazil) 1940. Damaged in 1962
182	(?)	No. 1	STA-Spl.	C4S/150	Mexican Air Force	As STM Six aircraft Invoiced 12-9-37
183	(?)	No. 2	STA-Spl.	C4S/150	Mexican Air Force	Same

ST Series Production

c/n	Date	Reg/No.	Model	Engine	Customer	History
184	(?)	No. 3	STA-Spl.	C4S/150	Mexican Air Force	J. Connolly (TN) NC7282C to NC17360 Flying '75
185	(?)	No. 4	STA-Spl.	C4S/150	Mexican Air Force	As STM
186	(?)	No. 5	STA-Spl.	C4S/150	Mexican Air Force	As STM
187	(?)	No. 6	STA-Spl.	C4S/150	Mexican Air Force	As STM MAF Sq. 203 Flying Club. Storage Ensenada 1975
188	5-10-38	NC18904	STA-Spl.	C4S/150	R. M. Genius*	Enclosed cockpit*. L. Russo (PA) Flying 1975
189	(?)	23	STA-Spl.	C4S/150	Honduran Air Force	As STM Invoiced 5-31-38
190	(?)	24	STA-Spl.	C4S/150	Honduran Air Force	Same
191	(?)	25	STA-Spl.	C4S/150	Honduran Air Force	Same
192	5-7-38	21	STA-Spl.	C4S/150	Guatemalan Air Force	As STM. F. Speck (PA). Rebuilding in 1975
193	5-7-38	22	STA-Spl.	C4S/150	Guatemalan Air Force	1975 in San Diego Aerospace Museum as NC14223
194	5-7-38	23	STA-Spl.	C4S/150	Guatemalan Air Force	As STM. History unknown.
195	5-7-38	24	STA-Spl.	C4S/150	Guatemalan Air Force	W. Hill (FL) Flying 1975 as NC17349
196	(?)	25	STA-Spl.	C4S/150	Guatemalan Air Force	History unknown
197	(?)	26	STA-Spl	C4S/150	Guatemalan Air Force	C/n & N49002 to NC17348 on PT-20 ? orig. c/n.
198	9-23-38	NC18902	STA	C4/125	Demorr Aviation	Don Cargill (MI) Flying 1975
199	10-31-38	NC18905	STA-Spl.	C4S/150	Gordon Barbour	Shipped to Bolivia.
200	10-31-38	NC18906	STA-Spl.	C4S/150	Ministro Defensa	Ecuador. History unknown

NOTE: The c/n range from 201 through 214 were assigned to SC series aircraft. No c/n from 215 through 299

c/n	Date	Reg/No.	Model	Engine	Customer	History
300	(?)	27	STA-Spl.	C4S/150	Guatemalan Air Force	As STM c/n 300 to 305 with gun mount on wings
301	(?)	28	STA-Spl.	C4S/150	Guatemalan Air Force	Same. Order invoiced 12-15-38 for c/n 300-305
302	12-15-38	29	STA-Spl.	C4S/150	Guatemalan Air Force	To USA. W Dodd (IL) N11D to N302D Flying '75
303	12-15-38	30	STA-Spl.	C4S/150	Guatemalan Air Force	Returned USA. F. Barber (GA) Rebuilding 1975
304	12-15-38	31	STA-Spl.	C4S/150	Guatemalan Air Force	To USA as N10535. R. Webb (FL) 1970 C.A.R.
305	(?)	32	STA-Spl.	C4S/150	Guatemalan Air Force	History unknown.
306	delivered 6-6-39 as	NC18907 39-717	STA XPT-16	C4/125	USAAC/1023 hr	First flight 2-3-39. STA became XPT-16. Modified to XPT-16A 1-7-41. Class 26 7-12-42
307	7-26-39	40-40	YPT-16	C4/125	USAAC/ 851 hr	To YPT-16A 2-13-41. Class 26 on 7-8-42
308	8-1-39	40-41	YPT-16	C4/125	USAAC/1077 hr	To YPT-16A 1-16-41. Class 26 on 7-31-42
309	8-1-39	40-42	YPT-16	C4/125	USAAC/ 681 hr	To YPT-16A 1-3-41. Collided PT-13 36-13 3-42
310	8-2-39	40-43	YPT-16	C4/125	USAAC/ 996 hr	To YPT-16A 2-17-41. Class 26 on 7-5-42
311	8-7-39	40-44	YPT-16	C4/125	USAAC/ 668 hr	To YPT-16A 4-18-41. Class 26 on 6-18-42
312	July 1939	NC18922	STA	C4/125	Ryan Aeronautical	Dick Woodson (CA). Flying 1975
313	7-31-39	40-45	YPT-16	C4/125	USAAC/ 936 hr	To YPT-16A 4-11-41. Gndloop Nov 41. Class 26
314	8-4-39	40-46	YPT-16	C4/125	USAAC/1269 hr	To YPT-16A 1-2-41. Class 26 on 7-10-42
315	8-3-39	40-47	YPT-16	C4/125	USAAC/1291 hr	To YPT-16A 1-7-41. Class 26 7-14-42
316	8-3-39	40-48	YPT-16	C4/125	USAAC/ 966 hr	To YPT-16A 1-30-41. Class 26 on 7-10-42
317	8-9-39	40-49	YPT-16	C4/125	USAAC/1071 hr	To YPT-16A 2-13-41. Posted Missing (?) date
318	8-14-39	40-50	YPT-16	C4/125	USAAC/1193 hr	To YPT-16A 2-3-41. Missing USA 11-31-43
319	8-11-39	40-51	YPT-16	C4/125	USAAC/ 479 hr	Wrecked 9-10-40 (never modified to YPT-16A)
320	8-7-39	40-52	YPT-16	C4/125	USAAC/ 985 hr	To YPT-16A 1-20-41. Class 26 1-13-43
321	8-14-39	40-54	YPT-16	C4/125	USAAC/1210 hr	To YPT-16A 1-23-41. Class 26 7-31-42
322	9-30-39	NC18923	STA	C4/125	Allan Hancock	J. M. Hoskin (WA). Flying 1975

STA c/n 149 N17346 -Dave Conoley

STA Special c/n 174 NC17369 -Leo Kohn

STM-2 c/n 467 with Gypsy engine

STM-2 c/n 465 with Lycoming -Hendon

PT-20's at Lindbergh Field -Ryan

STA c/n 128 as "radial" for movies -AAA

STA c/n 322 in 1960 as N18923 -E. Minta

STA c/n 166 NC17361 in 1967 -Burmister

STM - 1st Guatemalan order (no guns)

STM - 2nd order wing guns - note wrong star

12 Guatemalan STM in a row! -Ryan photos

Another rare shot, STM-2, STK, PT-20 -Ryan

Cockpit detail of PT-20 c/n 353   -Ryan

PT-20A classic flight shot by Bill Wagner

PT-20 portrait by Bill Wagner - Ryan

Mixed PT-16A and PT-20A -Ryan (Wagner)

ST Series Production

#	Date	Serial	Model	Engine	Owner/Hours	Disposition
323	12-12-39	40-2387	PT-20	L-365-1	USAAC/1123 hr	To PT-20A 12-12-40. Class 26 on 7-31-42
324	1-15-40	40-2388	PT-20	L-365-1	USAAC/1175 hr	To PT-20B. To PT-20A 4-23-41. Sold surplus '45
325	1-15-40	40-2389	PT-20	L-365-1	USAAC/1074 hr	To PT-20A 12-17-40. Hit power line 3-4-42
326	1-15-40	40-2390	PT-20	L-365-1	USAAC/1220 hr	To PT-20A 10-7-40. (?)
327	1-18-40	40-2391	PT-20	L-365-1	USAAC/1176 hr	PT-20A 10-15-40. Crash Mission Valley 2-5-42
328	1-22-40	40-2392	PT-20	L-365-1	USAAC/1286 hr	To PT-20A 10-16-40. Class 26 7-7-42
329	2-9-40	40-2393	PT-20	L-365-1	USAAC/1342 hr	To PT-20A 11-20-40. Class 26 7-7-42
330	2-12-40	40-2394	PT-20	L-365-1	USAAC/1104 hr	To PT-20A 12-17-40. (?)
331	2-13-40	40-2395	PT-20	L-365-1	USAAC/1231 hr	To PT-20A 11-22-40. Class 26 7-12-42
332	2-13-40	40-2396	PT-20	L-365-1	USAAC/ 728 hr	To PT-20B 1-20-41. To PT-20A 4-18-41. C.26
333	2-16-40	40-2397	PT-20	L-365-1	USAAC/ 856 hr	To PT-20A (No. 51) 11-22-40. Class 26 7-9-42
334	2-22-40	40-2398	PT-20	L-365-1	USAAC/1162 hr	To PT-20A 10-7-40. Class 26 7-22-42
335	3-7-40	40-2399	PT-20	L-365-1	USAAC/1140 hr	To PT-20A 10-29-40. Class 26 9-11-42
336	3-8-40	40-2400	PT-20	L-365-1	USAAC/1205 hr	To PT-20A 11-23-40. Class 26 10-11-43
337	delivered 3-12-40 as	NX18920 40-2401	STW PT-20	125 Warn. C4/125	Ryan Aeronautical USAAC/ 894 hr	Test for Warner. To Air Corps as PT-20. To PT-20A 11-20-40. Class 26 1-24-42
338	delivered 8-29-39 as	NX18919 40-53	STW YPT-16	Warner S50 C4/125	Ryan Aeronautical USAAC/ 653 hr	Test for Warner. To Air Corps as YPT-16 Hit H.T. Lines 9-18-40. Never a YPT-16A
339	7-11-39	NC18921	STA-Spl.	C4S/150	Demorr (dealer)	Mel Taylor (NY). Flying 1975
340	3-13-40	40-2402	PT-20	L-365-1	USAAC/ 617 hr	To PT-20A 11-20-40. Class 26 7-23-42
341	3-15-40	40-2403	PT-20	L-365-1	USAAC/1194 hr	To PT-20A 11-6-40. Class 26 7-14-42
342	3-22-40	40-2404	PT-20	L-365-1	USAAC/ 188 hr	Crashed before 8-26-40. Never PT-20A
343	3-26-40	40-2405	PT-20	L-365-1	USAAC/1170 hr	To PT-20A 11-20-40. Class 26 7-22-42
344	3-28-40	40-2406	PT-20	L-365-1	USAAC/1054 hr	To PT-20A 11-4-40. To School (Visalia) Class 26
345	3-30-40	40-2407	PT-20	L-365-1	USAAC/ 959 hr	To PT-20A 11-7-40. Crashed 11-18-41
346	4-3-40	40-2408	PT-20	L-365-1	USAAC/1063 hr	To PT-20A 9-26-40. Class 26 8-26-42
347	4-4-40	40-2409	PT-20	L-365-1	USAAC/ 648 hr	To PT-20A 10-29-40. Spun in 2-26-41
348	4-5-40	40-2410	PT-20	L-365-1	USAAC/ 971 hr	To PT-20A 10-14-40. Class 26 on 7-10-42
349	4-7-40	40-2411	PT-20	L-365-1	USAAC/ 852 hr	To PT-20A 12-2-40. Class 26 8-26-42
350	4-7-40	40-2412	PT-20	L-365-1	USAAC/1231 hr	To PT-20A 11-4-40. Class 26 8-26-42
351	4-8-40	40-2413	PT-20	L-365-1	USAAC/ 918 hr	To PT-20A 12-11-40. Class 26 7-8-42
352	4-8-40	40-2414	PT-20	L-365-1	USAAC/ 800 hr	PT-20A 12-13-40. F. Sorenson (CA) N69094
353	4-9-40	40-2415	PT-20	L-365-1	USAAC/ 893 hr	To PT-20A 12-17-40. Class 26 4-14-43
354	4-9-40	40-2416	PT-20	L-365-1	USAAC/ 298 hr	Wright Field. To PT-20A 10-24-40. Class 26 '43
355	3-16-40	NC9	STA	C4/125	C.A.A.	R France (VA) Stored good cond. 1969 as N9E
406	(?)	NX18924	STK	Kinner	Ryan Aeronautical	Test ship for Kinner B5. Disposition unknown

STM PRODUCTION FOR CHINA

356	STM-2E	1R	366	STM-2E	11R	376	STM-2P	21R	386	STM-2E	31R	396	STM-2E	41R
357	STM-2E	2R	367	STM-2E	12R	377	STM-2E	22R	387	STM-2E	32R	397	STM-2E	42R
358	STM-2E	3R	368	STM-2E	13R	378	STM-2E	23R	388	STM-2E	33R	398	STM-2E	43R
359	STM-2E	4R	369	STM-2E	14R	379	STM-2E	24R	389	STM-2E	34R	399	STM-2E	44R
360	STM-2E	5R	370	STM-2E	15R	380	STM-2E	25R	390	STM-2E	35R	400	STM-2E	45R
361	STM-2E	6R	371	STM-2E	16R	381	STM-2E	26R	391	STM-2E	36R	401	STM-2E	46R
362	STM-2E	7R	372	STM-2E	17R	382	STM-2E	27R	392	STM-2E	37R	402	STM-2E	47R
363	STM-2E	8R	373	STM-2E	18R	383	STM-2E	28R	393	STM-2E	38R	403	STM-2E	48R
364	STM-2E	9R	374	STM-2E	19R	384	STM-2E	29R	394	STM-2E	39R	404	STM-2E	49R
365	STM-2E	10R	375	STM-2P	20R	385	STM-2E	30R	395	STM-2E	40R	405	STM-2E	50R

1st S-T c/n 101 as X-14223   -Ryan

STA c/n 128 at Alameda, 1939-Bill Larkins

End of the line for c/n 164   -Mayborn

STA c/n 151 in original form   -Leo Kohn

STA c/n 177   -Dorr Carpenter

STA c/n 154 ex NC17351 as N633X -Ken Wilson

STM c/n 184 ex-Mexican AF -Carpenter

N17368 is not original c/n 173 but has been assigned its old number. Is really c/n 304.

ST Series Production

c/n	reg	A50	model	notes
407	RO-10		STM-2	NEI Army. Captured
408	RO-11		STM-2	NEI Army. Lost in war
409	RO-12		STM-2	NEI Army. Lost in war
410	RO-13		STM-2	NEI Army. Lost in war
411	RO-14		STM-2	NEI Army. Lost in war
412	RO-15		STM-2	NEI Army. Lost in war
413	RO-16		STM-2	NEI Army. Lost in war
414	RO-17		STM-2	NEI Army. Lost in war
415	RO-18		STM-2	NEI Army. Lost in war
416	RO-19		STM-2	NEI Army. Lost in war
417	RO-20		STM-2	NEI Army. Lost in war
418	RO-21		STM-2	NEI Army. Lost in war
419	RO-22		STM-2	NEI Army. Lost in war
420	RO-23		STM-2	NEI Army. Lost in war
421	RO-24		STM-2	NEI Army. Lost in war
422	RO-25		STM-2	NEI Army. Lost in war
423	RO-26		STM-2	NEI Army. Captured
424	RO-27		STM-2	NEI Army. Lost in war
425	RO-28		STM-2	NEI Army. Captured
426	RO-29		STM-2	NEI Army. Lost in war
427	RO-30		STM-2	NEI Army. Lost in war
428	RO-31		STM-2	NEI Army. Lost in war
429	RO-32		STM-2	NEI Army. Lost in war
430	RO-33		STM-2	NEI Army. Lost in war
431	RO-34		STM-2	NEI Army. Lost in war
432	RO-35		STM-2	NEI Army. Lost in war
433	RO-36		STM-2	NEI Army. Lost in war
434	RO-37		STM-2	NEI Army. Lost in war
435	RO-38		STM-2	NEI Army. Lost in war
436	RO-39		STM-2	NEI Army. Lost in war
437	RO-40		STM-2	NEI Army. Lost in war
438	RO-41		STM-2	NEI Army. Lost in war
439	RO-42		STM-2	NEI Army. Lost in war
440	RO-43		STM-2	NEI Army. Lost in war
441	RO-44		STM-2	NEI Army. Captured
442	RO-45		STM-2	NEI Army. Lost in war
443	RO-46		STM-2	NEI Army. Lost in war
444	RO-47		STM-2	NEI Army. Lost in war
445	RO-48		STM-2	NEI Army. Captured
446	RO-49		STM-2	NEI Army. Lost in war
447	S-11		STM-S2	NEI Navy. Lost in war
448	S-12		STM-S2	NEI Navy. Lost in war
449	S-13		STM-S2	NEI Navy. Lost in war
450	S-14	A50-7	STM-S2	NEI Navy. VH-AHF R. D. Soutar. Damaged 7-13-55 (?)
451	S-15	-	STM-S2	NEI Navy. Lost in war
452	S-16	(?)	STM-S2	NEI Navy. VH-AGY to VR-HDL to LN-TVF to N9761 J Bassett (IL) Stored '75 in WA.SA
453	S-17	A50-24	STM-S2	NEI Navy. Presently at Central Technical College, Brisbane, Australia
454	S-18	A50-27	STM-S2	NEI Navy. VH-AGU to VH-WEB A. Fisher. Wrecked 6-4-61. In storage 1975, Australia
455	S-19	A50-25	STM-S2	NEI Navy. Not sold surplus by RAAF.
456	S-20		STM-S2	NEI Navy. Lost in war
457	S-21	A50-30	STM-S2	NEI Navy. VH-BXN to VH-RUM to N8146 R. Friedman (IL) Flying 1975 in USA
458	S-22	A50-17	STM-S2	NEI Navy. VH-AGV to USA (unlicensed) K. Egger (OH). Stored '75
459	S-23	A50-11	STM-2	NEI Navy. VH-AGD I. B. Baille. Damaged February 1968. Rebuilding in 1975
460	S-24	A50-15	STM-2	NEI Navy. Not sold surplus by RAAF
461	S-25	A50-33	STM-2	NEI Navy. Not sold surplus by RAAF
462	S-26	A50-21	STM-2	NEI Navy. Not sold surplus by RAAF
463	S-27	A50-12	STM-2	NEI Navy. Not sold surplus by RAAF
464	S-28	A50-4	STM-2	NEI Navy. VH-ARR to VH-BNG to VH-RAF Robby Repair Ltd. Wrecked 6-8-52
465	S-29	A50-22	STM-2	NEI Navy. VH-AGW Colin Munk. Flying 1975 in Australia. Lycoming engine mod
466	S-30	A50-18	STM-2	NEI Navy. VH-BBJ. Dismantled, fuselage used on c/n 475.
467	S-31	A50-2	STM-2	NEI Navy. VH-AHS to VH-RAE. Flt. Lts Jeoffrey & Morty Susons, Rebuilding 1976
468	S-32	-	STM-2	NEI Navy. Lost in war
469	S-33	A50-34	STM-2	NEI Navy. VH-AHD Jess P. Trappett. Flying 1976 in Australia
470	S-34	-	STM-2	NEI Navy. Lost in war
471	S-35	A50-23	STM-2	NEI Navy. VH-BWQ David Bourke. Flying 1975 in Australia
472	S-36	-	STM-2	NEI Navy. Lost in war
473	S-37	A50-1	STM-2	NEI Navy. VH-AGQ being used with c/n 467 for one aircraft. Lts. J & M. Susons
474	S-38	A50-19	STM-2	NEI Navy. VH-AHE N. Hudson. Written off 1-27-56
475	S-39	A50-9	STM-2	NEI Navy. VH-AGR. L. Barnes. Crash 1948. Rebuilt from c/n 475 & 466. Flying '75
476	S-40	A50-31	STM-S2*	NEI Navy. VH-AGZ to N288Y to N7779 Mitch Mayborn. Flying 1975 USA. (* on nameplate)
477	S-41	A50-10	STM-2	NEI Navy. Not sold surplus by RAAF
478	S-42	-	STM-2	NEI Navy. Lost in war
479	S-43	-	STM-2	NEI Navy. Lost in war
480	S-44	-	STM-2	NEI Navy. Lost in war
481	S-45	A50-32	STM-2	NEI Navy. VH-AHA. Written off 11-25-49
482	S-46	(?)	STM-2	NEI Navy. VH-CXR A. Fisher. Flying 1975 in Australia with Gypsy engine mod
483	S-47	A50-5	STM-2	NEI Navy. VH-AGR. Wrecked 2-31-51. Registration reused.
484	S-48	A50-28	STM-2	NEI Navy. Scrapped for parts by RAAF 3-20-45
485	S-49	A50-14	STM-2	NEI Navy. Not sold surplus by RAAF
486	S-50	A50-16	STM-2	NEI Navy. Not sold surplus by RAAF
487	S-51	A50-8	STM-2	NEI Navy. Not sold surplus by RAAF
488	S-52	-	STM-2	NEI Navy. Lost in war
489	S-53	A50-13	STM-2	NEI Navy. VH-AGS to ZK-BEM Museum of Transport & Technology, Auckland, New Zealand
490	S-54	A50-26	STM-2	NEI Navy. VH-AGX to VR-HDM M. Hodkins (USA) Not registered
491	S-55	A50-20	STM-2	NEI Navy. Not sold surplus by RAAF
492	S-56	A50-29	STM-2	NEI Navy. VH-AHC V. T. Chapman. Flying 1975 in Australia
493	S-57	A50-6	STM-2	NEI Navy. VH-AGB C. Splatt. Written off 2-25-46
494	S-58	A50-3	STM-2	VH-AHG/VR-HDK/PI-C324/N14911 B. DeVries, USA as c/n 104.
495	RO-50		STM-2	NEI Army. Lost in war
496	RO-51		STM-2	NEI Army. Lost in war
497	RO-52		STM-2	NEI Army. Lost in war
498	RO-53		STM-2	NEI Army. Lost in war
499	RO-54		STM-2	NEI Army. Lost in war
500	RO-55		STM-2	NEI Army. Lost in war
501	RO-56		STM-2	NEI Army. Lost in war
502	RO-57		STM-2	NEI Army. Lost in war
503	RO-58		STM-2	NEI Army. Lost in war
504	RO-59		STM-2	NEI Army. Lost in war
505	RO-60		STM-2	NEI Army. Lost in war
506	RO-61		STM-2	NEI Army. Lost in war
507	RO-62		STM-2	NEI Army. Lost in war
508	RO-63		STM-2	NEI Army. Lost in war
509	RO-64		STM-2	NEI Army. Lost in war
510	RO-65		STM-2	NEI Army. Captured
511	RO-66		STM-2	NEI Army. Lost in war
512	RO-67		STM-2	NEI Army. Lost in war
513	RO-68		STM-2	NEI Army. Lost in war
514	RO-69		STM-2	NEI Army. Lost in war

SCW c/n 201 with Warner   -Ryan photo

"Dive brake" flaps (c/n 201) -Ryan photo

"Sisters" Menasco S-C and STA   -Ryan

T. Claude Ryan in c/n 201   -Ryan photo

c/n 204 in 1947 -William T. Larkins photo

c/n 202 NC18908 in late 1950's   -Mayborn

c/n 211, N46207   -Ken Wilson photo

c/n 208 in early 1940's   (Carpenter)

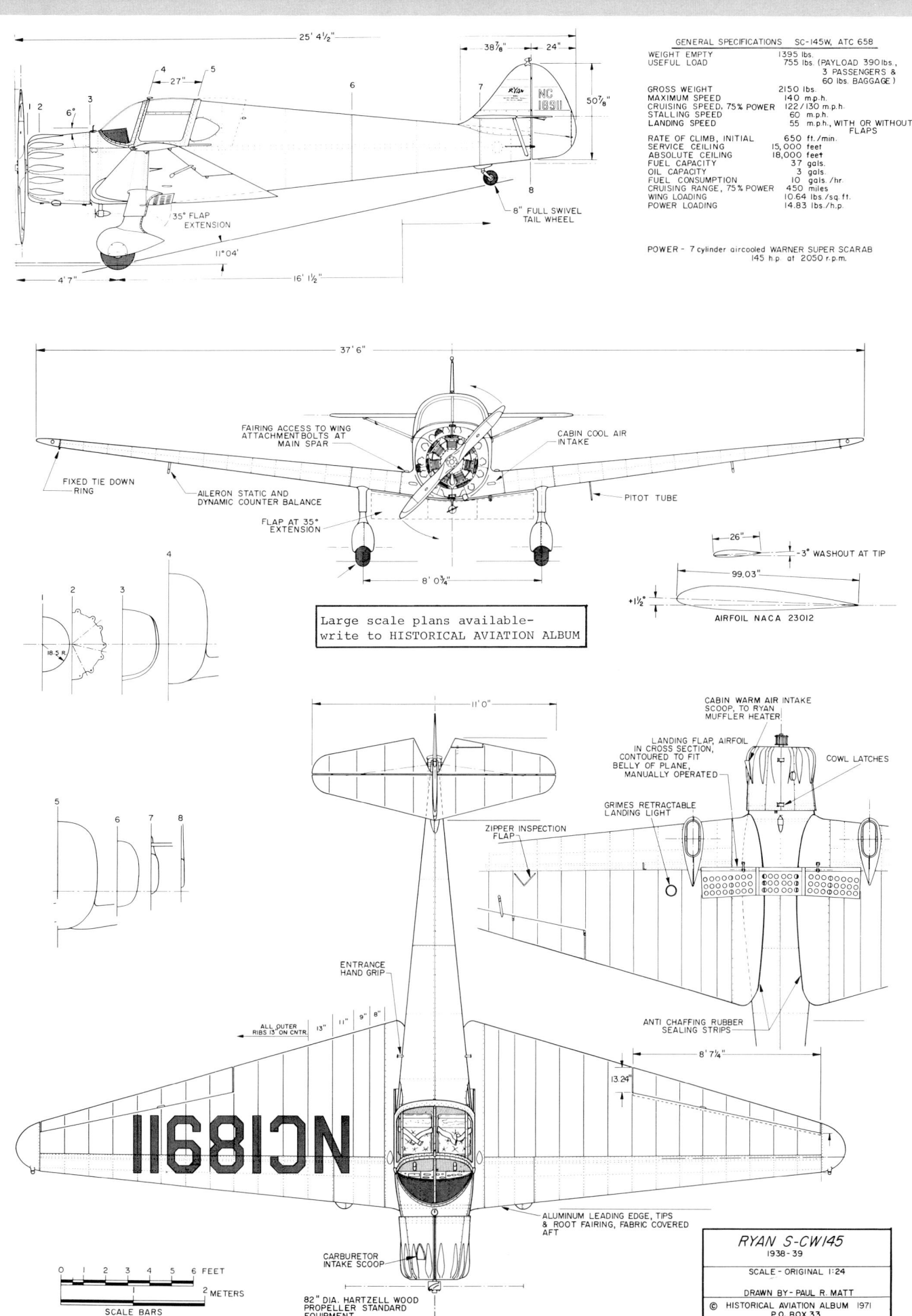

c/n 204, N18910   -John Underwood

c/n 205, N18911 with Lycoming -Underwood

c/n 206, NC18912   (Carpenter)

c/n 210, N18915 with 185 Warner -Mayborn

c/n 203, N18909   -Pete Bulban photo

Experimental "Dowty" gear.   -Ryan

CAP SCW with bomb on c/n 206.   -Ryan

Another SCW with bomb on patrol. -Ryan

RYANS IN MUSEUMS

Compiled by National Air & Space Museum (1975)

AIR FORCE MUSEUM (Dayton, Ohio)

PT-22 c/n 1750 AF s/n 41-15721 as N51713
X-13   AF s/n 54-1620

AIR MUSEUM (Chino, California - Ed Maloney)

FR-1 BuAer No. 39659 (storage)

AIRPOWER MUSEUM (Blakesburg, Iowa)

PT-22 c/n 2116 AF s/n 41-20907 as N48588
  on loan from D. Harrell

ARMY AVIATION MUSEUM (Ft. Rucker, Alabama)

VZ-3RY   AF s/n 56-6841
L-17A   s/n 47-1344

CONFEDERATE AIR FORCE

PT-22 c/n 1831 AF s/n 41-20622 an N22AL
  at Harlingen, Texas (flying condition).
PT-22 c/n 1298 AF s/n 41-15269 as N48742
  at Hobbs, New Mexico.

EAA AVIATION MUSEUM (Franklin, Wisconsin)

N.Y.P. (Replica) B.1 c/n 159 built by
  Paul Mantz in 1955.

HENRY FORD MUSEUM (Dearborn, Michigan)

N.Y.P. (Replica) B.1 c/n 156 donated by
  James Stewart (actor & USAF General)

JEFFERSON MEMORIAL MUSEUM (St. Louis, Mo.)

N.Y.P. (Replica) B.1 c/n 153 built by
  Paul Mantz. In storage.

MUSEUM OF TRANSPORT & TECHNOLOGY
  (Western Springs, Auckland, New Zealand)

STM-2 c/n 489 N.E.I. S-54 as ZK-BEM

NATIONAL AIR & SPACE MUSEUM (Washington, DC)

N.Y.P. Spirit of St. Louis c/n 30 N-X-211
X-13 AF s/n 54-1619

PIMA COUNTY AIR MUSEUM (Tucson, Arizona)

PT-22 c/n 1765 AF s/n 41-15736 as N1180C
  on loan from USAF Museum.

SAN DIEGO AERO SPACE MUSEUM (San Diego, CA)

M-1 c/n 23 NC2532
N.Y.P. (Replica) built by Frank Tallman
  M-1 fuselage framework used.
SCW c/n 204 N18910
STM c/n 193 painted as NC14223
PT-22 c/n 1419 AF s/n 41-15390
FR-1 BuAer 39707 on loan from NASM
XV-5A (mockup only) as 62-4505
X-13 (mockup only - storage)

SCW Production

c/n	Identification/Owner/Status
201	NX/NC17372 to XA-CUT to N18372, Morton Lester
202	NC18908, J. Steele. Flying 1975
203	NC18909 to N830E. E. M. Smith. Flying 1975
204	NC18910 in San Diego AeroSpace Museum, 1976
205	NC18911, Don Carter, flying 1976
206	NC18912, B. J. Larson, flying 1976
207	NC18913, destroyed by fire before 1951
208	NC18914, D. Barnard, flying 1976
209	PP-TEC. Shipped to Brazil, no further word.
210	NC18915 to N75395 to N147W to N18915 Dave Conoley, flying 1976 with 185 Warner.
211	NC18916 to AAF s/n 42-10742 as L-10, surplus to NC46207, King Egger, derelict in Houston Texas, 1976.
212	NC18917, Flint StSimons, 1945. Fate unknown
213	-Partial airframe only. Ryan School use.
214	C. J. Papas, built up airframe. Flying 1976

ARMY AIR CORPS SERIAL NUMBERS		
XPT-16	1	39-717
YPT-16	15	40-40/54
YO-51	3	40-703/705
PT-20	30	40-2386/2416
PT-21	100	41-1881/1980
PT-22	1023	41-15173/15745
PT-22	-	41-20591/21040
PT-22A	25	42-57479/57503
YPT-25	5	42-8703/8707

CORRELATION OF C/N WITH U. S. NAVY BUREAU OF AERONAUTICS NUMBERS - NR-1	
c/n	BuAer No.
1060	4099
1081/1154	4100/4173
1181/1205	4174/4198

THE ST-3 PT-21 PT-22 & NR-1

by Dorr B. Carpenter

A. K. Forest photo (Class 44E)

THE RYAN PT-22 was one of the best Primary Trainers of World War II. She was well built, strong, and of the same configuration as the period fighters (low wing monoplane). To train a fighter pilot or even to prepare him for the Basic and Advanced Trainers of the time was to give him his training in a flying brick. This was the Ryan PT-22.

Almost thirty-five years later, these planes still fly; over 200 are currently on the FAA register. The men who fly and know them realize that they are not stable at slow speeds. If you take her for what she is and fly her by the manual, you will have the time of your life. Because planes and parts are in good supply, the "22" is very popular with the sports flyer. In 1975, prices for flying planes range from $6000 to $8000. In the surplus market of 1946, they could be bought for $600 to $1000. The price did not start to go up sharply until the middle sixties when they averaged $2000 for a really good one.

The fuselage on the "22" is 14-in. longer and 3-in. wider than previous PT-16/PT-20 military models. Army adjustable seats were installed and the windshields were the familiar three section military type. Distance between wheels was increased by more than 12-in. by using knuckle-type wheel mountings instead of the fork previously used. Rudder design was altered to include the "clam shell" fairing as an integral part of the rudder. The baggage compartment was a canvas lined compartment on the left side of the tail cone, accessible only from the outside. Fuselage was an all metal monocoque construction, 39-in. high and 29-in. wide at the cockpit area. She has the same number of bulkheads (9) and the same number of skin sheets (6) of the same thickness as the earlier models, but the details of construction were heaver and geared for mass production. The wings were NACA 2412 airfoil section with a 3° incidence and 4° 30' dihedral. Structures consist of stub wings on either side of the fuselage, both with wing walks, and outer wing panels.

The stub wings were made of riveted aluminum skin and ribs with steel frame and cantilever aluminum rear spar. The wing panels had 13 stamped aluminum ribs and laminated spruce spars. The compression ribs were aluminum with five bays of drag and anti-drag wires. All flight surfaces were fabric covered and attachment was made with sheet metal screws. Tail surfaces were built from tubing and stamped ribs. One of the big differences in this model from the earlier planes was the use of ball bearings throughout. The tail wheel is steerable and mounts on an oil dampened shock strut. It becomes full swivel if the direction of the plane differs more than 45° from the rudder.

This model was never offered for sale new on the civilian market. In spite of the fact that articles were written about this ST-3 aircraft being equipped with engines other than the Kinner, none were built this way. One order was accepted by the Ryan Co. for ST-3 aircraft on floats equipped with the Menasco D4B engines, but none were delivered.

The ST-3, as the Ryan factory called her, was born out of necessity in the early 1940's. Her predecessors flew too well, and were too forgiving to the novice pilots. If one is going to fly a tricky plane like an Air Force fighter, there is no point in learning on an "easy to fly" airplane. The Army Air Corps realized this fact, and the early civilian ST design was redesigned to military specifications for the first time and modified with a sweep back to the wings of 4° 10' (to make it stall and spin). The end result was a superb military trainer.

These planes trained over 14,000 pilots for the Army and Navy during the war, yet more than half the planes survived the war. The aircraft were mostly based at Hemet and Palo Alto, California; Tucson, Arizona; Jacksonville, Florida; and Memphis, Tennessee.

The PT-21 and all the later Army models were painted the same: yellow wings and tail; red, white and blue rudder; natural aluminum fuselage, and U.S. Army in large block letters on only the underside of the wings.

The first contract was for PT-21 aircraft which were identical to the second prototype civilian ST-3KR (Sports Trainer, model 3 Kinner "R" series engine). These planes had fairings over the landing gear, but not the wheels, and the aileron counterbalance arms were on the underside of the wings. The engines, Kinner 132 hp (R-440-3) were delivered to the Army. Most were used at Palo Alto Field, King City, California. The landing gear fairings were removed shortly after they entered service.

The Republic of China received 70 PT-22 aircraft Lend-Lease in 1942. They were delivered via India and retained their U.S. markings until being delivered to China that same year. It is thought that most, if not all of these planes did not arrive in China.

The largest contract was for 1000 aircraft to be called the PT-22. These were basically the same as the first two models, but had a larger engine. This time the plane had a five cylinder radial with individually greased rocker arms (R-55 Kinner). This is the plane most flyers know and was called the "Recruit". There are no landing gear fairings and other than the engine and the placement of the aileron counterbalance arms on the top of the wing, it was the same as the earlier model. At a distance it became impossible to distinguish between the "21" and the "22" except by the Field numbers painted on the fuselage. The PT-21's had low "block type" numbers.

A number of years ago, I owned one of these planes. It was a "22", and its Army field number was 346. She was built in 1942, and used at Tucson, Arizona. All the Army records were still with her. In a total of 3200 hours of cadet flying and civilian use, there had been one landing accident involving a broken propellor. She had been fitted with five different Kinner R-540-1 and one R-540-3 engines. During the time I owned this ship, she had her last engine change with a major and modified R-540-3. She was destroyed in a fatal accident in August 1967.

The last production planes were PT-22C models. These had the Kinner engines of 160 hp with pressure lubricated rockers, and were called the R-540-3 (civilian nominclature R-56). There were 250 of these. Basically, the aircraft remained the same through the production of "21" and "22" models.

After the war, more than 500 of these aircraft were sold surplus. Most were destroyed, abandoned, junked and neglected during the next five years. The average pilot had a hard time flying them because of the high rate of sink, stall characteristics, and because she was "different" from any other single engine plane.

A good military trainer should be inexpensive, strong, easy to build, have the same configuration as the period fighters, and most importantly, have the same flying characteristics. The Ryan was all of these.

Checking Out

The flying idiosyncrasies were built into the aircraft mostly because of the added weight and the sweep back to the wings. If you are to fully understand this aircraft, a good long in-flight check out is a must. When at a high altitude, a number of maneuvers are recommended. Let the student set up a straight and level cruise RPM, and then start at 15° banked turn without adding power but holding altitude. You will get around about 250°, and the plane will stall and spin. The lesson learned is never to start a banked turn without adding power. The second maneuver could be a 720° turn at full RPM. Have the student slowly pull back the stick until she goes into a high speed stall. As the ship will stall at almost any speed or atitude if the "G" load is right, it is good to show the new pilot the feel of the Ryan just before she stalls. There is ample warning.

The third maneuver should be slow flight, controlling her roll only with the rudder. The "22" losses most of her aileron near stall speed and any cross controls of the aileron, near a stall, will result in a spin. The last maneuver is again slow flight, this time with flaps down and engine at idle, losing altitude as if landing. Dump the flaps suddenly and give her full power. The result is quite spectacular, if you are going slow enough she will snap roll and if not, she will sink about 100 feet before recovering.

This ship will do many things suddenly, but never without plenty of warning to a qualified pilot. When she spins, she is very easily recovered, but with the loss of a lot of altitude. In fact, she recovers so quickly that if you do not center your rudder precisely at the right moment, she will stop and spin in the other direciton.

One item that is quite perturbing to the new owner of a "22" is the sound she makes. Hold your head to one side of the cockpit, and then the other in flight. In every position the sound is different, from a smooth roar to sharp thuds. The reason for this is the 5 cylinder radial engine — an exhaust collector for the carburetor heat on one side and on the other side only 6-in. stacks.

The people who fly these PT-22 aircraft today seem to know their planes much better than twenty years ago. They really enjoy open cockpit flying and maintain them better than ever before and it shows.

In the years after World War II, many accidents befell the PT-22's, mostly because of poor maintenance, lack of understanding and little or no check out for the pilots. This resulted in a very bad reputation for the ST-3 Ryan. Mostly this reputation was not deserved. When writing about old airplanes, authors usually steered clear of talk about accidents. But in this case, we have listed all 65 major and minor accidents in PT-21 aircraft at King City, Calif. Palo Alto Field 1942. Remember these are young cadets with between 8 and 40 hours of flight time. The usual variables of weather, drinking, experience and equipment are eliminated.

Wind & Weather (on ground)	3	
Taxing	3	
Engine failure	5	
Take off	3	
Landing	25	(1)
Mid-Air	4	(2)
Off field crack ups	5	(1)
Out of gas	4	
Stall and Spins	3	
Airframe failure	2	(1)
Cause not reported	5	
	65	

(Indicates fatality)

If this aircraft is so dangerous, why were there only three stall spin accidents? The Army obviously could train low time cadets in the stall spin tendencies of the PT-22. Certainly, the modern high time pilots can learn — if they will listen. The landing accidents were mostly hard bounces and bad braking from inexperience and nothing that could

be attributed to the characteristics of the plane. The one landing fatality was when a student hit a pedestrian.

It is impossible to explain the airframe failure, as one was an elevator spar which could not have broken except in maybe a whip-stall, the other a broken landing gear possibly on a hard bound. With open cockpits and almost unrestricted visibility, it is hard to explain the mid-air collisions. Most of the other assorted problems were improper use of brakes and broken propellers.

N53071 c/n 1909 —Carpenter photo

N47306 c/n 1358 —Leo Kohn

N47081 to N246R c/n 1644 —Burton Kemp

N53118 c/n 1931 —Bill Larkins photo

N48307 c/n 1269 —Leo Kohn photo

N25510 c/n 1608 —Carpenter

N115H c/n 2032 with Ranger —Burton Kemp

N2022 (ex N53434) c/n 1054 —Carpenter

ST-3 Surplus Sales

The known civil registration is given in numerical order, the lowest number first (ignoring letter suffixes) in the left - hand column. The c/n is given followed by the military serial number and any remarks. To find original configuration compare c/n in list to the following table.

```
CONSTRUCTION NUMBER LIST OF ST-3 AIRCRAFT

1000-1001      ST-3 prototypes        2
1002-1059      PT-21                 58
1060           NR-1                   1
1061-1076      PT-21                 16
1077-1080      PT-22                  4
1081-1154      NR-1                  74
1155-1180      PT-21                 26
1181-1205      NR-1                  25
1206-1774      PT-22                569
1775-1799      PT-22A                25
1800-2248*     PT-22                450
                                   1250

*includes c/n 1979 and 1979A

NOTE: No PT-22B built
      PT-22C field modified to Kinner R-56
```

Surplus ST-3 tables list: "N" number, c/n, Air Corps serial, Remarks. Letters are: A-Active, W-Wrecked, S-Salvaged. D-Destroyed.

N	c/n	serial	Remarks
11X	1418	41-15389	-
22AL	1831	41-20622	A ex-54098
22JK	1697	41-15668	A ex-56139
78J	1682	41-15653	W '73
88E	2248	41-21040	ex 54012/to 883D
115H	2032	41-20823	A ex-53145, Cabin
170P	1566	41-15536	D '74 ex-60158
300RP	1031	41-1910	A Lyc R-680
343F	1580	41-15551	A ex-48310
246R	1644	41-15615	D (mod biplane)
262SR	1799	42-57503	A ex-48382
2860D	1178	41-1978	A
441V	1579	41-15550	A ex-59402
450	1641	41-15612	-
470S	1400	41-15371	W '65 ex-57913
487H	1868	41-20659	B ex-48773
579S	2062	41-20853	W '64 ex-57913
666K	1486	41-15457	D '64 ex-47211
721R	1840	41-20631	A ex-52509
780SR	2007	41-20798	A ex-46725
822PT	2130	41-20921	A ex-58667
883D	2248	41-21040	see 88E
1144	1887	41-20678	D '65 ex-52279
1180C	1765	41-15736	ex-54003
1243	2075	41-20866	W '65 ex-59450
1344	2086	41-20877	A (? W '70)
1616	1062	41-1941	ex-57030
2022	1054	41-1933	A ex-53434
2113	1645	41-15616	A ex-60154
4705	1400	-	W '65
7621	1969	41-20760	A ex-47621
18925	1000	civilian	1st ST-3 W
18926	1001	civilian	A as ST-3KR
25510	1608	41-15579	D '68
31687	1200	BN 4193	NR-1
38963	-	-	-
38964	1479	41-15450	A
38965	1677	41-15598	A blt 12-19-41
38966	2094	41-20885	-
38967	2151	41-20942	-
38984	-	-	-
38987	-	-	-
46158	141-	41-15381	-
46159	1463	41-15434	A
46160	-	-	-
46161	1925	41-20716	-
46162	2139	41-20930	-
46164	1420	41-15391	-
46165	1512	41-15483	-
46166	2229	41-21020	-
46167	-	-	-
46168	1998	41-20789	-
46170	2050	41-20841	A blt 3-42
46171	2227	41-21018	A
46176	1364	41-15335	W
46177	1416	41-15387	-
46178	2147	41-20938	D '63
46200	2202	41-20993	-
46208	1478	41-15449	-
46209	1954	-	-
46217	1363	41-15334	A blt 10-23-41
46218	-	-	-
46219	1743	41-15714	-
46220	1733	41-15704	D '65
46221	2189	41-20980	-
46230	1059	41-1938	-
46231	2082	41-20873	-
46232	2209	41-21000	-
46234	1074	41-1952	A
46500	2028	41-20819	-
46501	1777	42-57481	A
46502	1995	41-20786	A Ranger
46503	1290	41-15261	-
46504	1371	41-15342	-
46593	-	-	-
46596	1065	41-1944	-
46601	-	-	-
46604	1031	41-1910	to 300RP
46616	1262	41-15233	-
46685	1549	41-15520	A Lyc IO-360
46686	-	-	W 12-24-44
46687	1957	41-20748	-
46688	1860	41-20651	-
46698	-	-	-
46700	-	-	-
46701	1605	41-15576	W '64
46702	1606	41-15577	-
46703	-	-	-
46704	-	-	-
46705	1662	41-15633	W '73
46706	1717	41-15688	A
46707	-	-	-
46708	2077	41-20868	-
46709	-	-	-
46723	1686	41-15657	-
46724	1586	41-15557	-
46725	2007	41-20798	to N780SR
46726	-	-	-
46739	1011	41-1890	D '70
46740	1393	41-15364	-
46741	1439	41-15410	-
46742	1550	41-15521	-
46743	1660	41-15631	-
46744	-	-	-
46745	2131	41-20922	A blt 5-42
46746	2125	41-20917	-
46750	1307	41-15278	-
46751	2176	41-20967	W 9-12-73
46752	1375	41-15346	-
46753	1673	41-15644	-
46754	1958	41-20749	-
46792	1300	41-15271	-
46794	-	-	-
46795	1721	41-15692	A
46796	2052	41-20843	-
46804	1175	41-1975	D '66
46805	2015	41-20806	blt 3-28-42
46977	-	-	-
46984	1956	41-20747	-
46992	-	-	-
47010	1271	41-15242	-
47-11	1509	41-15480	-
47012	1685	41-15656	A
47013	-	-	-
47027	1400	41-15371	to 470S
47077	-	-	-
47078	-	-	-
47079	-	-	-
47080	1391	41-15362	A blt 10-31-41
47081	1644	41-15615	-
47082	1443	41-15414	A Ranger eng.
47094	1629	41-15600	-
47095	1256	41-15227	-
47096	1768	41-15739	-
47097	1460	41-15431	A
47105	2053	41-20844	-
47210	1292	41-15263	-
47211	1486	41-15457	-
47212	1511	41-15482	-
47213	1729	41-15700	-
47214	1820	41-20611	S '67
47306	1358	41-15329	A
47307	1607	41-15578	-
47308	1767	41-15738	-
47309	1808	41-20599	-
47310	1754	41-15725	-
47367	1675	41-15646	-
47368	1667	41-15638	W '73
47369	1668	41-15639	-
47370	1823	41-20614	D '58
47431	1362	41-15333	-
47432	1559	41-15530	A blt 12-6-41
47433	1719	41-15690	A
47434	1692	41-15663	-
47442	1392	41-15363	-
47443	1320	41-15291	-
47536	1303	41-15274	-
47537	-	-	-
47538	1707	41-15678	-
47539	1897	41-20688	-

NR-1 c/n 1129 with Ranger modification

N60155 c/n 2054 with 220 hp Cont. & hatch

N52456 c/n 1043 and STA N17361 c/n 166

N58667 c/n 2130   -Gregory Kohn

N11X c/n 1418   -AAA Archives

N48588 c/n 2116 in Arizona 1957   -Mayborn

N47027 c/n 1400 in 1955 -Carpenter photo

N52279 c/n 1887   -Carpenter photo

47540	2037	41-20828	
47541	1429	41-15400	A
47553	1514	41-15485	-
47554	1811	41-20602	D '72
47555	1928	41-20719	A blt 2-24-42
47556	1955	41-20746	A
47618	1581	41-15552	-
47619	1935	41-20726	-
47620	1857	41-20648	A blt 2-4-42
47621	1969	41-20760	A to 7621
47622	1979A	41-21040	? AF s/n
47623	1351	41-15322	D '65
47624	1789	42-57493	-
47708	1731	41-15702	-
47709	-	-	-
47713	1856	41-20647	-
47714	1879	41-20670	-
47840	1157	41-1957	A
47841	1979	41-20770	-
47842	1563	41-15534	-
47843	1901	41-20692	D '66
47844	1902	41-20693	-
47845	1929	41-20720	-
47846	1496	41-15467	-
47927	1529	41-15500	-
47928	1676	41-15647	A to CF-KTD
47929	-	-	-
47930	1917	41-20708	-
47931	1976	41-20767	-
47932	-	-	-
48015	1160	41-1960	-
48016	1492	41-15463	-
48017	-	-	-
48018	1561	41-15532	-
48104	1061	41-1940	-
48105	1977	41-20768	-
48106	1568	41-15539	-
48107	-	-	-
48108	1798	42-57502	-
48147	-	-	-
48148	1593	41-15564	-
48149	1261	41-15232	W '60
48155	1893	41-20684	-
48159	1848	41-20739	D '65
48234	2182	41-20973	-
48235	1903	41-20694	-
48236	1161	41-1961	-
48238	1569	41-15540	D '65
48306	1865	41-20656	-
48307	1268	41-15240	A
48308	1548	41-1551	-
48309	1578	41-15548	A
48310	1580	41-15551	to 343F
48330	1994	41-20785	-
48331	1821	41-20612	A blt 1-27-42
48332	2164	41-20955	-
48333	-	-	-
48381	1978	41-20769	S '66
48382	1799	42-57503	to N262S
48383	-	-	-
48384	1373	41-15344	-
48385	1636	41-15607	-
48457	1314	41-15285	-
48458	1072	41-1950	-
48459	1551	41-15522	-
48460	1565	41-15536	-
48461	1921	41-20612	-
48551	1962	41-20753	-
48552	1039	41-1918	Blt 6-6-41
48553	2160	41-20951	-
48554	1490	41-15461	-
48583	-	-	-
48586	-	-	S '64
48587	2073	41-20864	A
48588	2116	41-20907	AAA Museum
48593	1960	41-20751	-
48605	1585	41-15556	W '68
48606	1454	41-15425	W '66
48607	1577	41-15548	A
48608	1905	41-20696	A
48609	2222	41-21013	-
48700	1532	41-15503	A
48701	2101	41-20892	Blt 5-6-42
48702	2115	41-20906	-
48710	1260	41-15231	-
48711	1894	41-20685	S '64
48742	1298	41-15269	A
48743	1287	41-15253	A
48744	2041	41-20832	A
48745	2244	41-21035	-
48746	1787	42-57491	-
48747	1180	41-1980	A
48748	1683	41-15654	A bl5 1-7-42
48749	1402	41-15373	A
48750	1419	41-15390	-
48751	1305	41-15287	-
48752	1427	41-15398	A blt 11-8-41
48753	-	-	-
48754	1984	41-20775	-
48755	-	-	-
48756	-	-	-
48757	2072	41-20863	-
48758	1781	42-57485	D '68
48759	1497	41-15468	-
48760	1021	41-1900	S '64
48711	1923	41-20714	A
48772	2089	41-20880	A blt 5-23-42
48773	1868	41-20659	to N487H
48774	-	-	-
48775	-	-	--
48776	1390	41-15361	-
48777	1068	41-1946	A blt 6-41
48778	1057	41-1936	A
48799	2185	41-20976	-
48826	-	-	-
48827	2174	41-20965	W '60
48829	1890	41-20681	-
48830	1456	41-15427	-
48917	1876	41-20667	A
48928	2169	41-20960	Lyc O-435
48929	1900	41-20691	-
48930	1875	41-15487	-
48976	-	-	-
48995	-	-	-
48996	2181	41-20972	-
48997	1843	41-20634	-
49048	1987	41-20778	-
49049	1582	41-15553	A
49050	2096	41-20887	-
49082	1544	41-15515	D '67
49083	1850	41-20641	-
49084	2144	41-20935	-
49085	2145	41-20936	-
49086	1541	41-15512	A
49158	1291	41-15262	-
49159	1914	41-20705	-
49161	1951	41-20742	-
49162	2126	41-20917	-
49223	1014	41-1893	A blt 4-30-41
49656	1283	41-15254	-
49671	2212	41-21003	-
49674	1396	41-15367	A
49685	1051	41-1930	A blt 5-27-41
50644	1254	41-15225	A
50645	-	-	-
50646	1325	41-15296	-
50647	1801	41-20592	-
50648	-	-	-
50836	-	-	-
50837	-	-	-
50869	-	-	-
50870	1042	41-1921	-
50873	-	-	-
50875	-	-	-
50876	-	-	-
50878	-	-	-
50879	1735	41-15706	W '66
50880	1773	41-15744	-
50881	1853	41-20644	D '68
50882	1855	41-20646	-
50884	2183	41-20974	A blt 6-42
50885	2228	41-21019	A
50997	2240	41-21031	D '66
50916	-	-	-
50917	1278	41-15249	-
50918	1845	41-20636	-
50919	-	-	-
50920	1972	41-20763	-
50921	-	-	-
50993	2063	41-20854	A blt 4-24-42
50994	1779	42-57483	-
50998	1854	41-20645	W '68
50999	1464	41-15435	-
51029	-	-	-
51032	-	-	-
51035	2034	41-20995	A blt 6-42
51379	-	-	-
51707	1788	42-57492	A W '71
51708	-	-	-
51713	1750	41-15721	-
51726	-	-	-
51727	2060	41-20851	-
51728	1684	41-15655	-
51729	-	-	-
51730	1617	41-15588	-
52170	1609	41-15580	-
52257	-	-	-
52259	1661	41-15632	-
52279	1887	41-20678	to N1144
52280	1806	41-20597	S '66
52455	-	-	-
52456	1043	41-1922	W '73
52458	1394	41-15365	D '48
52459	-	-	-
52508	1895	41-20686	A
52509	1840	41-20631	to N721R
52670	-	-	-
52674	-	-	-
52676	-	-	-
52677	-	-	-
52689	-	-	-
52679	1418	41-15389	to N11X
52713	1284	41-15255	-
52724	1574	41-15545	W '67
53001	-	-	-
53003	1824	41-20615	-
53004	1888	41-20679	-
53005	2010	41-20801	-
53006	-	-	-
53007	1077	41-15173	D '67
53009	-	-	-
53010	-	-	-
53012	-	-	-
53013	-	-	-
53014	1500	41-15471	-
53015	-	-	-
53016	2186	41-20977	-
53-18	1164	41-1964	A blt 8-12-41
53020	-	-	-
53021	1701	41-15672	-

KINNER ENGINE NOMENCLATURE

B-5 (R-440-1)   125 hp at 1975 rpm   -   On ST-3 (as ST-3KB), STK, PT-20A, X/YPT-16A

B-54 132 hp - R-440-3 on PT-21   -   L-440-3 on NR-1

R-5 Series 2 - 160 hp on ST-3KR (c/n 1001, NX18926)

R-55 (R-540-1) 160 hp at 1850 rpm   -   On PT-22 and PT-22A

R-56 (R-540-3) 160 hp at 1850 rpm   -   On PT-22C (250 converted by Air Corps)

53022	-	-	-
53023	-	-	-
53071	1909	41-20700	A blt 2-22-42
53072	1828	41-20619	-
53073	2070	41-20861	-
53100	-	-	-
53106	-	-	-
53117	-	-	-
53118	1931	41-20722	-
53119	-	-	-
53120	-	-	-
53121	-	-	-
53138	-	-	-
53139	-	-	-
53140	1817	41-20608	-
43145	2032	41-20823	A
53146	2118	41-20909	A blt 5-11-42
53147	2019	41-20810	-
53149	2100	41-20891	A
53170	2107	41-20898	-
53171	1859	41-20650	-
53172	-	-	--
53173	2149	41-20940	-
53185	-	-	-
53186	1275	41-15246	-
53187	-	-	-
53188	1304	41-15275	-
53189	1265	41-15236	A blt 6-7-41
53190	1477	41-15448	A
53238	1940	41-20731	-
53271	1625	41-15596	A
53430	1822	41-20613	A
53431	1896	41-20687	A
53433	1810	41-20601	blt 1-25-42
53434	1054	41-1933	to N2022
53435	1961	41-20752	-
53437	1839	41-20630	W '74
43463	1680	41-15651	-
53496	1012	41-1891	-
53550	2194	41-20985	-
53551	-	-	-
53552	-	-	-
53789	-	-	-
53826	1522	41-15493	-
53998	1053	41-1932	A blt 2-28-41
5399	1162	41-1962	A blt 7-30-41
54000	-	-	-
54001	-	-	-
54002	-	-	-
53003	1765	41-15736	to N1180C
54004	1809	41-20600	-
54008	2066	41-20857	W '61
54010	-	-	-
54011	-	-	-
54012	2248	41-21039	to N88E
54014	2231	41-21022	-
54041	-	-	-
54046	2083	41-20874	D '63
54086	-	-	-
54098	1831	41-20622	to N22AL
54376	1289	41-15260	D blt 9-27-41
54377	1266	41-15237	-
54403	1387	41-15358	A
54428	2074	41-20865	W
54430	1728	41-15699	W '69
54446	-	-	-
54479	-	-	-
54480	1941	41-20732	A
54509	1840	41-20631	to N721R
54650	1584	41-15555	-
54660	1638	41-15609	-
54811	1861	41-20652	-
54817	1654	41-15625	-
54876	2097	41-20999	A blt 5-5-42
54907	2085	41-20876	A
54997	1299	41-15259	-
55046	-	-	-
55047	-	-	-
55048	-	-	-
55054	-	-	-
55061	-	-	-
55081	1422	41-15393	W '71
55082	-	-	-
55090	-	-	-

55093	-	-	-
55094	-	-	-
55095	-	-	-
55096	-	-	-
55478	-	-	-
56002	1761	41-15732	D½74
56006	1002	41-1881	A
56005	1663	41-15634	-
56007	2090	41-20991	-
56008	1691	41-15662	to CF-XNO
56017	1722	41-15693	A blt 1-13-42
56026	1652	41-15533	-
56027	1311	41-15282	-
56028	2014	41-20805	W '70
56029	-	-	-
56030	1752	41-15723	A
56034	1727	41-15498	A
56035	1446	41-15417	-
56037	-	-	-
56038	1308	41-15279	A blt 10-8-41
65045	2121	41-20912	-
56046	-	-	-
56047	2154	41-20945	A blt 5-19-42
56048	2220	41-21011	A
56049	-	-	-
56076	1309	41-15280	A
56081	1926	41-20717	A
56139	1697	41-15668	to N22JK
56202	1375	41-15346	-
56209	2234	41-21025	Lyc O-455
56243	1501	41-15472	-
56248	1517	41-15488	A
56253	1484	41-15455	W '67
56272	1296	41-15268	-
56299	-	-	-
56421	1539	41-15510	A
56434	1560	41-15531	A blt 12-6-41
56529	1744	41-15714	-
56534	1590	41-15561	A
56535	2146	41-20837	A blt 5-15-42
56564	1280	41-15251	-
56565	1431	41-15402	A
56653	2087	41-20878	S '64
56711	2084	41-20875	D '68
56727	-	-	S '64
56783	-	-	-
56792	1167	41-1942	-
56793	1071	41-1949	-
57008	2002	41-20793	-
57009	2059	41-20850	A blt 4-23-42
57010	-	-	-
57011	1794	42-57498	A
57014	-	-	-
57015	2042	41-20833	D '65
57016	1664	41-15635	W '64
57017	2106	41-20897	A blt 5-7-42
57023	-	-	-
57024	-	-	-
57025	-	-	-
57026	1764	41-15735	A
57027	1594	41-15565	A
57028	-	-	-
57029	-	-	-
57030	1062	41-1941	to N1616
57032	-	-	-
57034	1907	41-20698	D '62
57035	-	-	-
57036	-	-	-
57037	-	-	-
57040	-	-	-
57043	2152	41-20943	-

57053	2215	41-21006	-
57080	1698	41-15669	blt 1-9-42
57081	1505	41-15476	W '68
57084	-	-	-
57085	2136	41-20827	A blt 5-14-42
57098	-	-	-
57165	1259	41-15230	A blt 9-12-41
57170	1755	41-15726	to CF-JLX
57182	2046	41-20837	A
57184	1306	41-15277	A blt 10-7-41
57185	1766	41-15737	W '72
57188	2057	41-20848	A
57264	1599	41-15570	A
57426	1301	41-15272	-
57427	1918	41-20709	-
57428	1705	41-15676	-
57627	-	-	-
57628	2205	41-20996	-
57882	1558	41-15529	-
57904	-	-	-
57905	-	-	-
57906	1526	41-15497	W '67
57908	-	-	-
57911	1602	41-15573	A blt 12-17-41
57912	1711	41-15682	A blt 1-12-42
57913	2062	41-20853	to N579S
57914	2086	41-20877	to N1344
57915	-	-	-
57919	-	-	-
58076	1066	41-1945	-
58083	-	-	-
58184	-	-	-
58188	-	-	-
58612	1716	41-15687	A blt 4-12-42
58614	1448	41-15419	-
58651	1426	41-15397	W '74
58667	2130	41-20921	to N822PT
58729	1277	41-15248	Cont. 220 hp
59220	2058	41-20849	A blt 12-9-42
58402	1579	41-15550	to N441V
59411	1366	41-15337	A
59417	-	-	-
59418	2169	41-20959	A
59450	2075	41-20866	to N1243
59466	1604	41-15575	A blt 12-41
59502	1293	41-15264	A
59505	1412	41-15383	A
59514	1991	41-20782	W '73
60150	-	-	-
60151	-	-	-
60152	-	-	-
60153	-	-	-
60154	1645	41-15616	A
60155	2056	41-20847	A Cont. W-670
60156	1413	41-15384	-
60157	1282	41-15253	to N99994
60158	1566	41-15537	to N170P
60159	-	-	-
60160	-	-	-
60161	1751	41-15722	-
60170	1596	41-15567	W '72
60178	2184	41-20975	A
60179	1272	41-15243	blt 9-16-41
60231	2005	41-20796	A
60488	1032	41-1911	A
60805	2175	41-20966	A
61005	1591	41-15562	A blt 12-41
61646	1612	41-15583	A
61647	2078	41-20869	A
61747	1491	41-15462	D '65
61883	1774	41-15745	A
62130	1812	41-20603	A
66622	1129	BN4148	A Ranger (NR-1)
67640	-	-	NR-1
73729	1643	41-15614	-
88717	1433	41-15404	D '64
99994	1282	41-15253	ex-60157

CANADIAN ST-3

CF-KTC	1676	41-15647	ex N47928
CF-JLX	1755	41-15726	D '67 ex N57170
CF-HFR	1556	41-15527	-
CF-XNO	1691	41-15662	ex N56008

The BONEYARD. Ogden Utah 1955 -Mayborn

NX18925 c/n 1000   -Ryan (Wagner) photo

Ring cowl on c/n 1000   -Ryan photo

Front view of c/n 1000's ring cowl -Ryan

The first NR-1 c/n 1060   -Ryan photo

Early PT-21   -Ryan photo

Pair of PT-21 in formation   -Ryan photo

Seven more PT-21   -Ryan (Wagner) photo

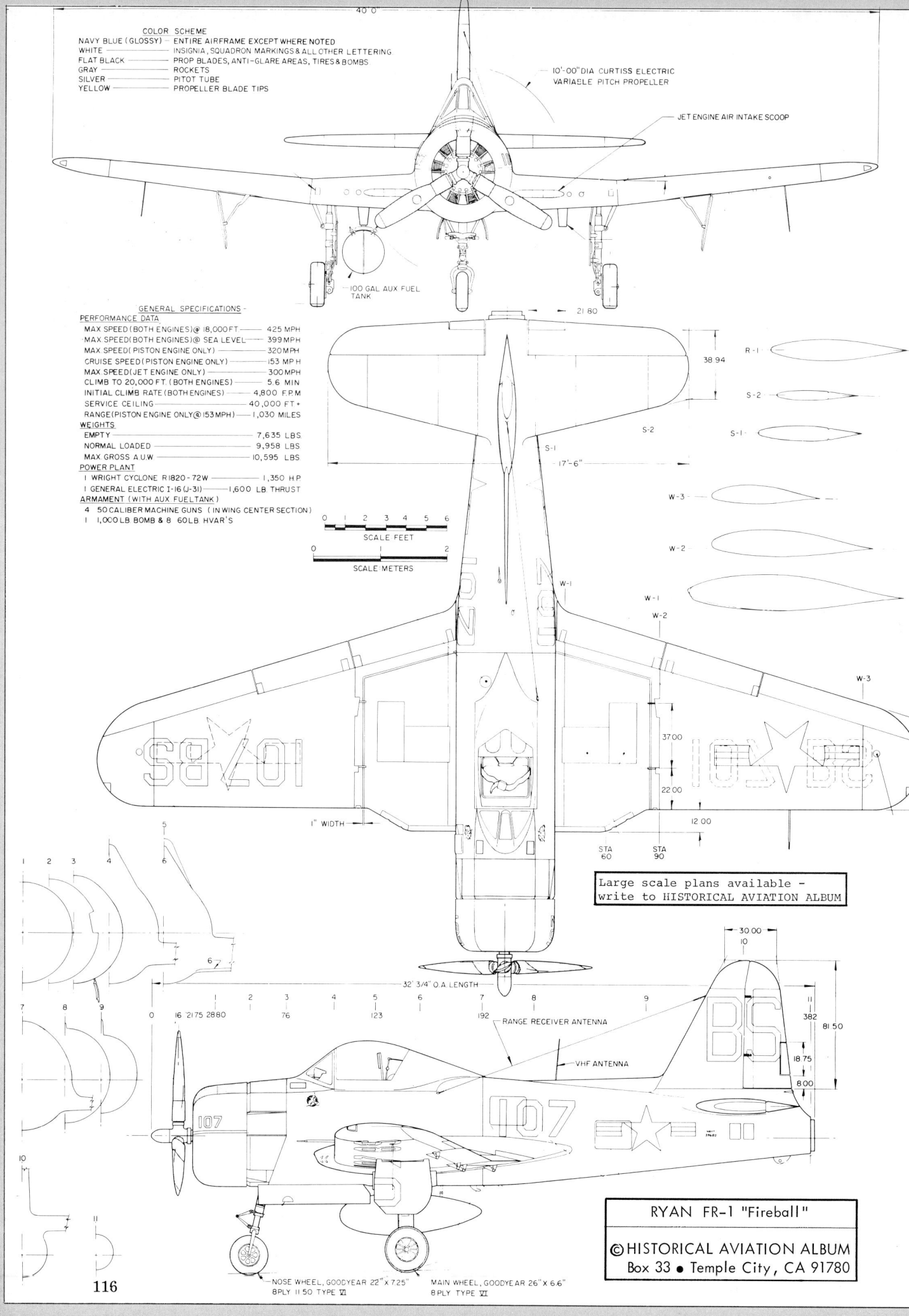

Forced landing

No. 368 - Stalled on first solo

No. 91 - Forced landing

No. 182 - Undershot the field

No. 195 - Undershot the field

No. 355 - Bounced, stalled and turned over

On landing No. 411 collided with No. 310

No. 48 forced landing

YPT-25 in flight   -Ryan photo

Taxiing the YPT-25, note background

Ryan Navion - Super 260   -Ryan photo

Ryan Navion - Super 260 (1952) Bill Larkins

Surplus L-17B c/n NAV-4-1731   -Larkins

L-17B Army 48-933 in 1955   -Bill Larkins

Navion 205 and L-17B AF 48-1060 -Ryan

VZ-3RY in second configuration-Ryan photo

PERFORMANCE & SPECIFICATIONS

MODEL	PRICE	CLASS	ENGINE & HP	SPAN	LENGTH	HEIGHT	EMPTY WEIGHT	GROSS WEIGHT	VMX	VCR	SERVICE CEILING	St. Miles RANGE
M-1	-	3POLM	Hisso 150 hp	36'	24'	-	1550	2700	125	110	15,000	400
M-1/M-2	$7400	3POLM	J-4B 200 hp	36'	24'	-	1600	2800	135	115	17,000	500
B.1	$9700/$12,200	5PCLM	J-5C 220 hp	42'	27'9"	9'10"	1870	3300	125	105	16,000	700
N.Y.P.	$20,580	1PCLM	J-5C 223 hp	46'	27'7"	9'10"	2150	5250	130	105	-	4110
B.1X	gift	6PCLM	J-5 200 hp	46'	27'9"	9'10"	2000	3600	126	100	-	-
B.3	$12,250	6PCLM	J-5C 200 hp	42'4"	28'3"	9'10"	2114	3704	125	105	15,500	700
B.5	$13,500	6PCLM	J-6-9 300 hp	42'4"	28'3"	9'10"	2250	4000	138	112	18,000	750
B7	$16,985	6PCLM	Wasp 420 hp	42'4"	29'11"	9'9"	2503	4283	150	120	20,000	600
C1	$10,900	4PCLM	J-6-7 225 hp	39'3"	27'7"	8'6"	2000	3300	130	110	16,000	650
S-T	$3585 '35	2POLM	B4 95hp	30'	21'5½"	6'11"	1023	1575	140	120	15,500	400
STA	$4685 '36	2POLM	C4 125 hp	30'	21'5½"	6'11"	1023	1575	150	127	17,500	350
STA Spl.	$5185 '37	2POLM	C4S 150 hp	30'	21'5½"	6'11"	1058	1575	160	135	21,000	350
YPT-16	$6380	2POLM	C4 125 hp	30'	21'5½"	6'8½"	1100	1600	150	127	17,500	350
PT-20	$6380	2POLM	C4 125 hp	30'	21'5½"	6'8½"	1093	1600	150	127	17,500	350
YPT-16A	-	2POLM	B5 125 hp	30'	20'11½"	6'8½"	-	1600	134	-	-	-
PT-20A	-	2POLM	B5 125 hp	30'	20'11½"	6'8½"	-	1650	134	-	-	-
STM-2	-	2POLM	C4S 150 hp	29'11"	21'5½"	6'11"	1096	1600	-	-	-	-
STM-S2	-	2POL/SM	C4S 150 hp	29'11"	22'8½"	7'4½"	1311	1828	122	108	12,250	246
PT-21 NR-1	-	2POLM	B54 132 hp	30'1"	22'5"	6'10"	1278	1825	123	112	11,900	340
PT-22	-	2POLM	R55 160 hp	30'1"	22'7½"	7'2"	1313	1860	131	123	15,500	352
YPT-25	-	2POLM	O-435 185 hp	32'10½"	24'3"	6'8"	-	1800	149	134	20,300	378
YO-51	-	2POLM	R985 420 hp	52'	34'5½"	11'1"	-	4206	130	32	-	-
S-C	-	3PCLM	C4S 150 hp	37'6"	26'7"	7'						
SCW	$6885	3PCLM	SS-50 145 hp	37'6"	25'4½"	7'	1350	2150	152	136	19,400	520
FR-1	-	1PCLM	R1830 1350 hp J-31 1600 st.	40'	32'1"	13'11"	7635	10,595	425	152 prop	43,100	1620
Navion A (205/L-17)	-	4PCLM	E185 205 hp	33'5"	27'6"	8'8"	1782	2750	163	155	15,600	500
Navion B (260)	-	4PCLM	GO-435 260 hp	33'5"	27'6"	8'8"	1782	2850	174	170	18,000	415
X-13	-	1PCLM	Avon 10M st.	21'	24'	15'	-	7500	-	-	-	-
VZ-3RY	-	1PC/OLM	T53 1000 shp	23'5"	27'8"	10'8"	-	2600	-	0	-	-

STA c/n 312 - top speed 150   -Mayborn

S-T c/n 102 - top speed 140   -G. Williams

X-13 with wheels in vertical flight -Ryan

X-13 with wheels in horizontal take-off

FR-1 on jet engine alone   -Ryan photo

Front view FR-1 with rockets and jet only

FR-1 BuAer 39703 1946 VF41 -Bill Larkins

VZ-3RY in third configuration -Ryan photo

Proposed Ranger powered Ryan trainer

Chinese STM-2P with machine gun -Ryan